"William Edgar's *A Supreme Love* stands as something of a tour through the story of jazz and all that has shaped and informed it. After a solid introductory chapter called 'Jazz and the Gospel,' Edgar takes the reader through a tour of slavery, the churches, the spirituals, the blues, gospel, and all the social, religious, and musical forces that coalesced in the development of jazz—a tour that runs for nearly half his book. But that's Edgar's way, as he doesn't want to rush too quickly past all those formative voices and influences, such that when he arrives at the point where jazz music begins to be formed, the reader is ready to roll. Newcomers to this music will find a deep and useful introduction to the music, with footnotes filled with links to online samples. Jazz fans will enjoy the tour, quibbling from time to time as to why this artist or that album wasn't cited . . . which is something jazz fans love to do! Read and be enriched."

Jamie Howison, author of *God's Mind in That Music: Theological Explorations Through the Music of John Coltrane*

"In my musician mind there has always been a deep connection between jazz, musical improvisation, and the disciple life. To risk the creation of improvised music armed with only imagination and talent is to dive right in to the center of grace. It's in the grace of God through Jesus that the musician finds peace, receives love that casts out fear, and learns to trust the reconciling power of the gospel to turn every misspent note into a glorious tool of orchestration. I simply don't know of any contemporary who has mined this field more than Bill Edgar. With *A Supreme Love*, the gifted Dr. Edgar invites all readers from every vocation to experience what he's known and taught for decades now: Jesus and jazz are inextricably linked."

Charlie Peacock, Grammy Award–winning music producer and founder of the commercial music program at Lipscomb University

"Once in a while a theologian tips the hand and reveals their passions unrelated to their professional pursuits. Karl Barth wrote on Mozart, and William Edgar, respected theologian at Westminster Theological Seminary, has written *A Supreme Love*, paying homage to his passion for jazz. A competent practitioner of the art form throughout his life, he puns on Coltrane's *A Love Supreme* for the title of his book. The result: a mature theologian's thinking that generates a sophisticated and personal account of the historical sweep of jazz history through the lens of a performer who has had a rich life of interacting with luminaries in jazz history. A delightful read for many who would be both theology-inclined readers and lovers of the arts who might not necessarily bring jazz into the conversation. For those who enjoy both passions, this book's for you. May this book always appeal to the intellectually curious, not least to those interested in theology and jazz history."

Johann Buis, musicologist, Wheaton College

"Art is surprisingly adept at finding beauty in the paradoxes and tensions of Christian faith, and jazz music is a particularly potent genre in this regard. William Edgar's *A Supreme Love* is a lovely reflection on the ways jazz and the gospel can converse. Edgar offers a welcome example of sophisticated theological engagement with music, without feeling forced. I learned so much reading this book—and discovered some great music too!"

Brett McCracken, senior editor at the Gospel Coalition and author of *The Wisdom Pyramid: Feeding Your Soul in a Post-Truth World*

"With love and verve, Bill Edgar describes jazz—the movement from deep misery to unspeakable joy—not only as the gift of the creativity and hard-won faith of Black artists, but also as a reflection of the racial and musical complexity of America. Read the book and listen to the music (on the links Edgar provides) with gratitude to these Black artists and the loving God who inspired them."

William Dyrness, senior professor of theology and culture at Fuller Theological Seminary and author of *The Facts on the Ground: A Wisdom Theology of Culture*

"For many years, Bill Edgar has been a leading figure in the music and theology world. Here he shows how deeply intertwined jazz is with the Christian gospel. But not only does he have an impressive grasp of his subject; he is a practitioner par excellence. This double qualification means that anything he writes deserves to be listened to with special care."

Jeremy Begbie, Duke University

"It is evident on every page that this is a labor of great love, informed by a lifetime of listening to and performing jazz music. Bill Edgar gives particular attention to the ways that jazz reflects the profound suffering and the extraordinary strength of the African American community. It is just this history, he argues, that gives rise to a music that enacts a gospel-shaped movement from sorrow to joy."

Steven R. Guthrie, professor of theology and religion and the arts at Belmont University

"Jazz pianist Professor Edgar shows convincingly how jazz is rooted in the African American Black experience of daily persecuted suffering and Sunday jubilation. The biblical faith of spirituals and the psalm-like lament of blues constitute the very fiber of jazz. That is why jazz music can move from expressing deep misery to ending with sounds of inextinguishable joy. This well-written book has verve, is effortlessly informed, and offers a treasury of websites and books for anyone who wishes to understand and enjoy the gift of jazz."

Calvin Seerveld, professor emeritus of philosophical aesthetics at the Toronto Institute for Christian Studies

WILLIAM EDGAR

A
SUPREME
LOVE

THE MUSIC
OF JAZZ AND THE
HOPE OF THE GOSPEL

Foreword by **CARL ELLIS** and **KAREN ELLIS**

ivp
Academic

An imprint of InterVarsity Press
Downers Grove, Illinois

InterVarsity Press
P.O. Box 1400 | Downers Grove, IL 60515-1426
ivpress.com | email@ivpress.com

InterVarsity Press® is the publishing division of InterVarsity Christian Fellowship/USA®. For more information,
visit intervarsity.org.

Scripture quotations, unless otherwise noted, are from The Holy Bible, English Standard Version,
copyright © 2001 by Crossway Bibles, a division of Good News Publishers. Used by permission. All rights reserved.

Cover design and image composite: David Fassett

Interior design: Jeanna Wiggins

ISBN 978-1-5140-0066-3 (print) | ISBN 978-1-5140-0067-0 (digital)

Printed in the United States of America ♾

Library of Congress Cataloging-in-Publication Data
Names: Edgar, William, 1944- author.
Title: A supreme love : the music of jazz and the hope of the gospel /
  William Edgar.
Description: Downers Grove, IL : IVP Academic, [2022] | Includes
  bibliographical references and index.
Identifiers: LCCN 2022009694 (print) | LCCN 2022009695 (ebook) | ISBN
  9781514000663 (print) | ISBN 9781514000670 (digital)
Subjects: LCSH: Jazz–Religious aspects–Christianity. | African
  Americans–Music–Religious aspects–Christianity. | African
  Americans–Religion–History.
Classification: LCC ML3921.8.J39 E35 2022 (print) | LCC ML3921.8.J39
  (ebook) | DDC 201/.678165–dc23
LC record available at https://lccn.loc.gov/2022009694
LC ebook record available at https://lccn.loc.gov/2022009695

26 25 24 23 22 | 6 5 4 3 2

TO MY DEAR FRIENDS

Monty and Caterina Alexander,

who personify the music described in these pages

CONTENTS

PART III: JAZZ MUSIC

FOREWORD

CARL ELLIS AND KAREN ELLIS

If you've ever spent time around William Edgar as he perches sideways on a piano bench, you may have heard him describe himself as "a jazz musician disguised as a theologian." Once he turns from teaching to the keys, what at first seems like self-deprecation soon becomes crystal clear: he is a master jazz theologian, and the two identities are in perfect harmony, serving the depths of our humanity with the touch of God; indeed, jazz music is from the soul, of the soul, and for the soul.

We experience life in parallels: the formal and the dynamic, unity and diversity, form and freedom, the one and the many, and on and on. Great thinkers throughout history have wrestled with these parallels, asking, "Which one prevails in our reality?" From God's limitless perspective, two realities can fulfill, harmonize, and dance with each other because they are creations of the unlimited Being, namely, God himself.

Musically, these dimensions can be expressed in terms of classical (formal) and jazz (dynamic). In the larger Western context, the expression developed on the formal side, while in the African American context, the expression was birthed from the dynamic side. Representing much more than a musical form, jazz emerged from a facet of life marked by improvisation within a theme. Taking this into the classroom of life, the classical dimension provides useful parameters for doing theology, while the jazz approach empowers us with wisdom to live out that theology in the rapidly shifting context of life.

Then there's the blues, jazz's country cousin who paints mental pictures of reality, not merely concepts. Ol' Cousin Blues slides up from the Mississippi Delta to help us not just understand but to *feel* life it as it evokes real memories from our experiences. The blues parallels the stormy relationship between God and his covenant people. When sung from a man's perspective, the blues is usually about a wayward woman—his significant other. What better illustration is there between God and his unfaithful people? The divine blues theme is the song of Hosea, a brother whose wife violated her marriage covenant in every conceivable way, leading to prostitution and slavery. Despite her ways, Hosea redeemed her because of his passionate love for her. God expresses his passionate redeeming love in the blues refrain:

> How can I give you up, Ephraim?
>   How can I hand you over, Israel?
>
> How can I treat you like Admah?
>   How can I make you like Zeboyim?
>
> My heart is changed within me;
>   all my compassion is aroused.
>
> I will not carry out my fierce anger,
>   nor will I devastate Ephraim again. (Hos 11:8-9 NIV)

When sung from a woman's perspective, the blues is usually about her lover, who is unfaithful and cruel, an excellent picture of how idols treat people. She longs for true love but only finds heartbreak, and only God can satisfy her deepest longing, making promises beyond the imagination, and keeping them all . . . such is the song of God.

God's ever-refreshing mercies expose in brilliant, high-fidelity surround sound the multilayered jazz dimension of the hope of the gospel of Christ. It's the cultural offering borne of the eternal surprising us in the temporal, and it's a lyrical prayer to a God who was resisted in all other places of life. It's the syncopation of eternity dancing on the soil of the temporal, and it's the return of the soul dynamic to the one who created it. The author writes that he hopes this book will "persuade the reader that the music cannot be properly understood without some familiarity with the Christian message. This does not mean one must be a theologian to grasp the message. But it will help to know the basics of creation, the fall into sin, and the redemption of all things by the grace of God. These basic tenets find their way into jazz." From where we sit, it takes a peculiarly gifted person to coax that message out of the horn, to tickle it out of the keys, to slap it out of the bass, and beat it out of the drum. It takes a jazz musician disguised as a theologian.

It takes a humble master-teacher such as William Edgar.

ACKNOWLEDGMENTS

This book is a labor of love. I have spent years reflecting on the meaning of jazz. I want to thank some of the many who have helped through the gestation and up to the birth of these pages. My editors at InterVarsity Press represent the gold standard. I am especially indebted to my publishing supervisor and friend, David McNutt. He has guided me through each stage of the process with dedication. Many of the ideas have been tested through him, and through friends who were willing to have a look at them and render their honest critiques. Special thanks are also due to Jeffrey Monk for creating the indexes.

I also want to thank my employer, Westminster Theological Seminary, for believing in the project, and giving me the time to develop it. I particularly want to thank my wife, Barbara, for her patient care throughout.

Strength and dignity are her clothing,
    and she laughs at the time to come.
She opens her mouth with wisdom,
    and the teaching of kindness is on her tongue. (Prov 31:25-26)

INTRODUCTION

JAZZ AND THE GOSPEL

Jazz washes away the dust of everyday life.

ART BLAKEY

It has been my privilege to grow up with jazz, to study it, and to perform it. I am not a headliner, but I'm a decent amateur. Once, at a fundraising concert in New York City, I had the privilege of being in a quartet with the great John Patitucci on bass, an extraordinary saxophone player, Joe Salzano, and the irrepressible vocalist Ruth Naomi Floyd.[1] After listening to the recording, my friend Monty Alexander said, "Wow, you kept up with big guys." That's as high a compliment as I've ever received, and from one of the greatest pianists on the planet.

Not everyone can be an aficionado. But it is my conviction that jazz is one of the most enjoyable and meaningful kinds of music there is. My friend Ted Turnau recounts how he "fell in love" with jazz: "When I listened to that music, my heart soared. The guitar solos, the piano solos, the harmonies, the bass lines, the rhythms—all of it seemed full of a

---

[1]Chesterton House, "Ground Zero, Jazz & Heaven," *Chesterton House* (blog), March 13, 2007, https://chestertonhouse.org/blog/ground-zero-jazz-heaven/.

shimmering, transcendent joy that I had a hard time defining."[2] One of my hopes is that after reading this book, more readers will become listeners and be convinced at least to give it a chance.

This music comes from the African American experience. Jazz is America's original music. Born out of slavery, it was nurtured in the invisible and visible churches where spirituals were generated, in the cotton fields with their inhuman working conditions, in the night spots across the country, and in funeral processions where dirges were followed by jubilation. Much of it has great depth, often the tragic sounds of suffering, but also of great jubilation. Because of its compelling beauty it has become popular all over the world. Thus, a style of music generated in relatively obscure circumstances has made it to stages all around the globe.

It became extraordinarily popular in the 1920s. At least one novelist who attempted a depiction of jazz did so by describing the period, or the *era*, which produced it. F. Scott Fitzgerald eloquently wrote of the "jazz age" in a manner that led many people to think he had invented the word. He had not. Jazz had been around before World War I, but what he did was manage to capture the spirit of the decade between the end of the war and the stock market crash of 1929. Somehow the word jazz was one appropriate metaphor for that time.[3]

Jazz is a great treasure of human civilization, and it appeals to people across cultural and religious differences. And yet I believe that it owes a great deal to a Christian worldview, which is deeply embedded in its origins and ongoing history. My claim is not made in order to justify liking the music, even less vindicating it as somehow acceptable for all believers. Rather, I want to advocate for this extraordinary music that is deeply informed by Christian convictions. In my view, jazz is best understood in light of the gospel. Both the sorrow and the joy found in jazz resonate with the deep pain and the incredible hope that stand at the heart of the Christian faith.

---

[2]Ted Turnau, *Pop-ologetics: Popular Culture in Christian Perspective* (Phillipsburg, NJ: P&R, 2012), 42-43.

[3]See particularly F. Scott Fitzgerald, *Tales of the Jazz Age* (New York: Vintage Classics, 2010), and of course *The Great Gatsby*, where jazz is featured throughout (New York: Scribner, 2004).

WHAT IS JAZZ?

The locals in New Orleans called it a "funeral with music." That's because the more popular label "the *jazz* funeral" doesn't tell the whole story. The term jazz did not even appear in print until 1919, although it was likely used orally before then.[4] Jazz music was often heard in these New Orleans funeral processions, but originally they included more than jazz—there was European "classical" music, African ritual sounds, the church's spiritual songs, and much more. Typically the parade was led by a soldier holding a sword, then a few ministers, followed by the coffin, with pallbearers, then a brass band, and finally family and friends.[5]

Figure I.1. The New Orleans "jazz funeral" moves participants from mourning to joy.

---

[4]A good deal of speculation exists as to the origins of the word. One of the best summaries of the research is Alan P. Merriam and Fradley H. Garner, "Jazz—the Word," in *The Jazz Cadence of American Culture*, ed. Robert G. O'Meally (New York: Columbia University Press, 1999), 7-31.

[5]An early account by a White traveler is Benjamin Latrobe, *The Journal of Latrobe: The Notes and Sketches of an Architect, Naturalist and Traveler in the United States from 1796 to 1820* (New York: D. Appleton, 1905), 180-82. See also R. Collins, *New Orleans Jazz: A Revised History* (New York: Vintage, 1996), 122-26.

As they processed toward the cemetery, which was on the edge of town, the music was slow and mournful. Frequent tunes included *Hark from the Tomb* or *We're a Marching to the Grave*. Then, when the body was interred, the band would light up with a joyful sound. They might play *When the Saints* or the slightly irreverent *Didn't He Ramble*.[6] The great pianist and pioneer of jazz Ferdinand "Jelly Roll" Morton once explained, "Rejoice at the death and cry at the birth: New Orleans sticks close to the Scriptures."[7]

Defining jazz is not as simple as it may seem. When asked to offer his definition, Louis Armstrong, the extraordinary New Orleans trumpet player, famously quipped (perhaps unkindly), "Man, if you gotta ask you'll never know."[8] We can take comfort in the "agnosticism" of certain scholars. In a thoughtful article, venerable musicologists Alan P. Merriam and Fradley H. Garner sought to identify the exact source for this word. After exploring the most likely origins, including peoples' names, foreign trans-literations, different cities, and salacious connotations, they came to the following conclusion: "We suggest the need for linguistic and philological research although we are not at all sure that the origin of jazz, the word, can ever be found."[9] That may be true for the word, but still, most people recognize the music.

It should be noted that a number of jazz musicians don't like the term. The outstanding jazz composer and orchestra leader Duke Ellington famously objected to it because he felt it pigeonholed the music into a predictable genre, and also because to him it had racial overtones. He is supposed to have said, "In the end there are only two kinds of music, good and the other kind."

Whatever the precise etymology of the word, any definition of jazz must account for its historical context. The French jazz advocate and critic Hugues Panassié defined jazz as "music created by Black people from the

---

[6]See Eileen Southern, *The Music of Black Americans: A History* (New York: Norton, 1971), 343.
[7]Marshall Bowden, "Jazzitude.com - U. S. Internet Magazine," Jazz Crusade Audio Sampler Catalog, accessed December 26, 2021, www.jazzcrusade.com/JCCD/JC3062.html.
[8]From Max Jones et al., "Salute to Satchmo" (London: IPC, 1970), 25. There is evidence that what he really said was, even more unkindly, "If you still have to ask, shame on you."
[9]Jones et al., "Salute to Satchmo," 28.

United States, taking its origins from the religious and secular music of Black Americans."[10] Our definition and articulation of jazz will need to take this historical context into account for it cannot be understood without it. And yet jazz is more than its history.

YOU BLOWS WHO YOU IS

As a genre, jazz resists definition, and yet there are identifiable aspects to jazz. Panassié argued that jazz included three essential ingredients: swing, the application of Black vocal technique to instruments, and melodic and harmonic qualities from the blues.[11] The best jazz preserves the personal style of a musician while yet participating in these conventions. When I listen to jazz, I can usually tell within a few measures who is playing, just from the distinctive style a musician brings to the instrument. Louis Armstrong once commented, "What we play is life." And he added, about the trumpet, "You blows who you is."[12]

Let's look at five characteristics of this music.

(1) Jazz has simple but significant formal qualities. A few technical considerations are in order here. Jazz was rarely notated, at first. Nevertheless, we can try to transcribe it with notes and measures. In the standard Western way of putting things onto a score, the basic rhythmic unit is the measure. Most music, whether jazz or not, comprises a certain number of measures. Measures typically contain either three or four beats. Often the standard jazz piece has the format AABA. Each of these comprises eight measures, totaling thirty-two. The beginning is called the "head." The B section is the "bridge," which has contrasting material from the three A sections. It may help to think of a standard song, such as *I Got Rhythm* by George Gershwin: This song has three A sections, two at the beginning and one at the end. The B section comes between the first two As and the

---

[10]Hugues Panassié and Madeleine Gauthier, *Dictionnaire du Jazz*, new ed. (Paris: Albin Michel, 1980), 167-71.

[11]Panassié and Madeleine Gauthier, *Dictionnaire du Jazz*, 167-71.

[12]See David Kunian, "You Blows Who You Is: Louis Armstrong Embodied the Folksy Sophistication That Marks New Orleans," *OffBeat*, July 28, 2016, www.offbeat.com/articles /blows-louis-armstrong-embodied-folksy-sophistication-marks-new-orleans/.

last one: A, A, B, A. The A section ("I got rhythm . . .") uses the standard chord progression C-A-D-G (in the key of C). "I Got Rhythm" is typically in Bb (thus, Bb-G-C-F). This progression is found in thousands of pieces, both jazz and classical. Then comes the contrasting B section ("Old man trouble . . ."), known as the bridge. In this song, the progression is another standard pattern known as the cycle of fifths (E-A-D-G in the key of C, or D-G-C-F in the "Rhythm" key of Bb). The pattern of this particular song is so common that musicians call it "rhythm changes" meaning the chords and the measures that characterize this song are found in many others (a *change* is a jazz term for a chord of harmony).

The other form that typically characterizes jazz is the blues. Here, the standard pattern is twelve measures, not thirty-two. And the structure is a bit different. It is an A (four measures), a B (four measures), and finally a C (four measures). For musicians, the standard changes (harmonies) are I (the tonic), IV (the subdominant), finally V (the dominant), and back to I (tonic again). For convenience, let's take the key of C. The tonic is the C chord, the subdominant is the F chord and the dominant is the G chord. The blues can be played in any key, and the chord patterns represent the same sequences.

Knowing about these patterns explains why musicians who have never met or played together can so seamlessly perform with one another and be on the same page. Jazz also makes extensive use of the "blues scale," which uses a good many flatted thirds, flatted fifths, and sevenths, often bending them the way a guitarist can do. Melodies are expressive, using leaps into falsetto and grace notes.[13]

(2) Importantly, jazz music is improvised. This term needs unpacking. Many people, when they first hear this term, imagine a musician taking off into unchartered territory, playing what he feels like, with few rules to guide him. This view is quite erroneous. It is true that jazz allows for considerable freedom, but it always takes place within a form. The form may vary, but it is usually a set number of harmonies (musicians call them "changes") over

---

[13]For an excellent introduction to the way jazz works formally, you might consider Gary Giddens and Scott DeVeaux, *Jazz* (New York: W. W. Norton, 2009), 1-41.

a particular rhythm. The best musicians tell a story, using those changes as a guide. In a group of musicians, improvisation is like conversation. Much as in the use of language and gestures in an animated discussion, there are thousands of ways of articulating the chords, playing with their basic nature, using falsetto and bending the notes, or creating countermelodies or even substitute chords to enhance the story. You can get the idea from a great rendition of *C Jam Blues*, a Duke Ellington piece, played by the wonderful pianist Oscar Peterson and his trio.[14] After a long solo piano blues, the trio kicks in, never too far from the simple pattern of the blues with occasional chord substitutions. The bass joins in and then things build and build, with Oscar's unique licks, interspersed with well-chosen call-and-responses, and finally back to the "head" (the tune, which is a single note in the key of C). Words can hardly describe the intensity, the interplay between the musicians, the creative blues patterns. But it is jazz.

Jazz is primarily derived from a way of singing born in the African American context, wherein the notes are stretched and bent to express passion. Jazz is closely tied not only to the blues, with its passionate use of perfusion and stretched notes but to the dance, and hence possesses what has become called "swing," a special kind of rhythm not found in quite the same way in other music.

(3) Jazz is not a single style, frozen in time. Jazz evolved from various kinds of folk music, together with more structured compositions, such as ragtime, and the composite became a truly unique art form. This synthesis occurred in the early years of the twentieth century. It is in fact one of the "miracles" of the history of music. From the barrel houses and churches to the concert stage, jazz moved from local expressions to become a world-renowned genre. It varies from disparate performances to sophisticated compositions, and even masterpieces. Jazz, with all its variety, has become a universally recognized family.

(4) Importantly, jazz is a music of protest. If we take stock of the blues, the spirituals, and many other forerunners to jazz, we see that they carry

---

[14]"Oscar Peterson - C Jam Blues," YouTube video, 9:06, posted by "dgbailey777," December 13, 2010, www.youtube.com/watch?v=NTJhHn-TuDY.

a spirit of protest. Spirituals are "sorrow songs," as W. E. B. Du Bois called them.[15] The blues carry an undertone of trouble and sadness, but they are also songs of defiance at the dehumanizing conditions of slavery, the struggles under Jim Crow legislation following emancipation, and the injustices that Black communities continue to face. The extraordinary Frederick Douglass, who poignantly described the life of a slave, wrote this about the effect of spirituals on his understanding:

> They told a tale of woe which was then altogether beyond my feeble comprehension; they were tones loud, long, and deep; they breathed the prayer and complaint of souls boiling over with the bitterest anguish. Every tone was a testimony against slavery, and a prayer to God for deliverance from chains. The hearing of those wild notes always depressed my spirit, and filled me with ineffable sadness. I have frequently found myself in tears while hearing them. The mere recurrence to those songs, even now, afflicts me; and while I am writing these lines, an expression of feeling has already found its way down my cheek. To those songs I trace my first glimmering conception of the dehumanizing character of slavery.[16]

This phrase "every tone a testimony" is telling.[17] Douglass calls these sounds a testimony to the horrors of slavery, but he also acknowledges them as prayers, and so he considers them ultimately hopeful. Good jazz should lead the listener from the tribulations of suffering into great joy. Not every piece contains this full narrative, but the whole body of jazz does. As the psalmist proclaimed, "You have turned my mourning into dancing" (Ps 30:11).

(5) Jazz can be very deep, even probing. Some jazz critics fault the music for its simplicity. There is, to be sure, simple, unchallenging jazz.

---

[15]W. E. B. Du Bois, *The Souls of Black Folk* (Chicago: A. C. McLung, 1903), 116-17.

[16]Frederick Douglass, *Narrative of the Life of Frederick Douglass, an American Slave* (New York: Simon & Brown, 2013), 14.

[17]The phrase was selected as the title for the recordings and accompanying booklet produced by the Smithsonian Folkway Recordings, an anthology of African American voices from the early days of recording technology to the present. It is an excellent introduction to the Black experience through the sounds it generated: Folkways Catalog number SFW47003 (2001).

But the best of it is rich in rhythmic complexity, instrumentation, variations on a theme, and melodic profundity. Some pieces are deceptively simple. Take, for example, Duke Ellington's *Mood Indigo* (1930). The instrumentation is unique: a trumpet, a trombone, and a clarinet. And, unusually, the clarinet is playing the low register and the trombone the melody. Scholars have suggested this unique voicing produces a "phantom" harmonic presence, making it sound as though there were a fourth player at the microphone.[18]

Many artists are masters at driving their music toward more and more intensity. I will never forget a performance by Jay "Hootie" McShann of "Swingin' the Blues" at the Montauban Jazz Festival back in 1983. It must have lasted twenty minutes or longer. It kept building and building until we all thought we would burst. When it did not seem possible to add to the passion if one more chorus were introduced, introduced it was, with even greater intensity. We were swept away.

But jazz can also be quiet and profound. Once, in a jazz band where I was the pianist, we were at a rehearsal. We were practicing the New Orleans classic "Some of These Days." After we finished there was a moment of respectful silence; we were all deeply moved. Then someone said: "Mozart!" We all nodded and smiled. This is difficult to describe in words, but we felt it had melodic invention and simple chord progression as in some of Mozart's music, albeit in a jazz idiom. There may be a parallel to this in the visual arts. Jazz drummer Elvin Jones once said, "I can see forms and shapes in my mind when I solo, just as a painter can see forms and shapes when he starts painting. And I see different colors."[19]

So jazz articulates a particular aesthetic. Growing out of the "funeral with music," jazz articulates a narrative which *moves from deep misery to inextinguishable joy.* Perhaps such an aesthetic could apply to all sorts of musical traditions and styles. But jazz does it in a unique way. One of them is to reflect the dance movements associated with spirituals and

---

[18]Brian Zimmerman, "Duke Ellington—'Mood Indigo,'" Song of the Day, *Jazziz*, April 29, 2019, www.jazziz.com/duke-ellington-mood-indigo/.

[19]Whitney Balliett, "Profiles: A Walk to the Park," *The New Yorker* (May 18, 1968), 60.

blues among Black people, both of which are different from the typical European styles. Many dance practices of African Americans evoke what Zora Neale Hurston calls "dynamic suggestion." That is, as she puts it, while the White dancer attempts a complete, classical expression, "the Negro is restrained, but succeeds in gripping the beholder by forcing him to finish the action the performer suggests."[20] She is saying that Black dancing draws people in, involving them in a performance. Surely too sharp a distinction should not be made, but the element of "dynamic suggestion" is an important feature of Black music.

With this working definition and these characteristics in mind, the following considerations will be simply divided into three major sections. First, the historical background of jazz and how it emerged within the context of slavery. Second, the key feeders that led to jazz, including field hollers, work songs, spirituals, gospel, blues, and ragtime. Third, the particular features of jazz music, its contours, and especially the relationship between jazz and the Christian message. The relation between jazz and the gospel message is somewhat intangible, though it is present at many levels. Both are realistic about the dark side of life. Both tell us how to navigate some of its vicissitudes: the gospel through its practical spirituality, and jazz through its improvisation. And both express hope at some level. To borrow from some of the great spirituals, like the gospel, jazz gives you "strength to climb."

I will make every attempt to interact with the music itself. I write as an academic, but one whose passion for jazz is nearly unbounded, perhaps second only to my passion for my faith in Christ. I hope the reader can feel this.

AESTHETICS, CULTURE, AND HISTORY

This study focuses on aesthetics. Let me try to unpack that notion. *Aesthetics* as a term and a category of philosophical reflection was first developed by A. G. Baumgarten in the eighteenth century, but of course

---

[20]Zora Neale Hurston, "Characteristics of Negro Expression," *The Jazz Cadence of American Culture*, ed. Robert G. O'Meally (New York: Columbia University Press, 1998), 302.

the experience of aesthetics predated his term. Broadly speaking, aesthetics has to do with perception, though it is often equated with our views of art.

If we follow the Christian philosopher and neo-Calvinist Calvin Seerveld, we would associate aesthetics with things that bring joy. Aesthetics, he tells us, is "an irreducible ordinance God laid down for creatures to follow, a creaturely dimension with ludic structure, one way we exist characterized by nuancefulness; a window on joy."[21] Seerveld has spent a lifetime wrestling with questions about aesthetics. Among his other useful contributions is his calling into question the careless way many people associate *beauty* with a kind of Platonic sense of harmony, balance, and congruence. In this view, something beautiful here below is mimetic (an imitation) of a higher design. Certainly many philosophers, Christian and otherwise, have gone down this path. The pioneering Dutch scholar H. R. R. Rookmaaker, for example, diagnoses the "death of a culture" by looking at paintings that lead toward fragmentation.[22] His younger friend and fellow Kuyperian philosopher, Calvin Seerveld, takes a different tack. There are two problems with beauty-as-harmony, argues Seerveld. One is that it imposes a category that might be foreign to the object in question. Is the image on an old Persian manuscript well understood if it qualifies as beautiful? The other problem is that some art is purposefully violent or ugly. For example, African tribal masks are meant to convey the threat of evil forces. They ought not be beautiful in any Platonic sense if they are to be believed.[23]

I find this critique helpful. At the same time, however, I don't think that aesthetics must *always* reflect joy or the ludic. For example, is not Francisco Goya's *Third of May, 1808*, which depicts the point-blank murder of Spanish resistance forces by Napoleon's firing squad, aesthetically

---

[21]Calvin G. Seerveld, "Joy, Style, and Aesthetic Imperatives," in *Normative Aesthetics*, ed. John H. Kok (Sioux Center, IA: Dordt College Press, 2014), 108.

[22]Calvin Seerveld, *Rainbows for the Fallen World* (Toronto: Tuppence, 2005), 121-25.

[23]Seerveld, *Rainbows*, 154-55.

powerful and successful? Yet there is no joy in it at all. According to philosopher Bence Nanay, aesthetics is tied to the natural world. In his words, aesthetics is about "our experience of breathtaking landscapes or the pattern of shadows on the wall opposite your office."[24] For him, aesthetics is mostly affirmative and often tied to natural beauty. For me, all quality aesthetics need not be connected to nature.

In my view, aesthetics is more about values than abstract statements of what constitutes beauty. An aesthetic quality is an artful way to understand a particular narrative. To be sure, music is clearly not a philosophy text in sound. Anyone who has struggled with expressing in words what a particular piece may mean, even if that piece itself has a text, knows the difficulty of doing so. Yet, at another level, music, like other art forms, does articulate meaning, a meaning that may at least partially be translated into words. That is because it is generated by human beings. The meaning may be from many sources, including a composer's mind or soul, a cultural context, a tradition, a worldview, or a social function.

Aesthetics is also closely related to craft. This connection was recognized in biblical times. The Old Testament dedicates considerable space to descriptions of skilled artists. Bezalel and Oholiab were specially called by the Lord to help build the tabernacle. Bezalel was endued with God's Spirit, enabling him "with ability and intelligence, with knowledge and all craftsmanship, to devise artistic designs" (Ex 31:3-4). Similarly, Solomon hired the Gentile Hiram to craft many features of his temple. He was "full of wisdom, understanding, and skill for making any work in bronze" (1 Kings 7:14). This relation is specifically indicated for music. Over and over the Old Testament especially heralds playing an instrument "skillfully" (Ps 33:3; 1 Sam 16:16-18). The "opposite" of such playing is deemed "noise" (see Amos 5:23).

But biblical aesthetics is much more than a few skilled artists designing buildings or playing stringed instruments. Consider the artistic ways in

---

[24]Bence Nanay, *Aesthetics: A Very Short Introduction* (Oxford: Oxford University Press, 2019), 4.

which authors portray people and events. Matthew alternates stories of miracles with discourses. The author of Jonah uses metaphors about descending and ascending in an artistic way. He also highlights the role of plants and other living things in the drama of Jonah's spiritual obduracy. Again, the psalms powerfully depict the heights and depths of human experience through matchless poetry. The sheer length of Job's so-called friends' speeches is an artistic device to show their pigheadedness. The Bible is full of aesthetic references because that is part of the warp and woof of human existence. We are aesthetic creatures. The conviction expressed in this book is that the aesthetics of jazz cannot be understood without acknowledging the reality of the biblical God who is present, often implicitly, in the life and music of Black people to give strength in time of need.

There are several questions that one might ask or observations one might make about jazz from the perspective of aesthetics.

First, very simply, does this music please? The ability to please is often mentioned in definitions of aesthetics and art. Every now and then I do encounter folks who say they do not like jazz. That's fine, depending on their reasons. Some people just do not know the music. Others imagine it is something it is not. Still others use the dubious category of "highbrow vs. lowbrow," or worse, the racist notion that jazz is the music of "barbaric" people. I hope the present volume at least clears away the cobwebs.

Second, aesthetics is about power. I want to argue that good jazz music has power. The ultimate source of that power, as I see it, is what we might call the *jazz narrative*, or the *African American aesthetic*, which is a movement from deep misery to inextinguishable joy. That narrative owes a great deal to the biblical gospel. I will not be suggesting that jazz is necessarily *Christian* music, whatever such a label might mean. Instead, I will argue that this music is in an important way explicable because of a Christian consciousness. I am well aware that there are voices besides the biblical witness that animate this music. I am also aware that a degree of secularism has made its way into Black thought. But as historian Vincent W. Lloyd argues, even in the voices of those who have turned against the Christian faith, such as James Baldwin and Malcolm X, their prophetic stance is filled with biblical cognizance.[25] I find that resonance with the Christian faith deeply embedded within jazz.

Third, there is a powerful relation between music and the soul. The philosopher Friedrich Nietzsche once declared: "Without music life would be a mistake." He added, "I could only believe in a God who danced."[26] In my jazz band, we like to add another phrase to this: "we could only believe in a God who knows suffering." Many have reflected on the sacred aspect of music. Mickey Hart once said: "[Music] has many sides. It can seduce or frighten you. It can rattle your bones. It can let you see God."[27] And Mark Helprin has a particularly felicitous phrase in one of his novels: "If it weren't for music, I would think that love is mortal."[28]

Fourth, aesthetics takes note of the historical and cultural background of each genre. All music is interwoven with history and culture. This is patently the case with the music of African American people. Some critics would be uncomfortable identifying a distinctive African American *aesthetic* because they believe music is universal. Yet while every people group has music, there is something special about each one. In the case of jazz, the music was shaped into a discrete art form because of its creators, refusing to dignify their music or paint with the category we call art. While it most certainly is an art, we don't want it to blend in with the romantic notion of art as sublime. This is to ignore both the root and the fruit, and the origins we briefly mentioned. The root, because it is a glorious art, but an art hammered out on the anvil of a long and troubled history. The great novelist Toni Morrison said, "Black Americans were sustained and healed and nurtured by the translation of their experience

---

[25]Vincent W. Lloyd, *Religion of the Field Negro: On Black Secularism and Black Theology* (New York: Fordham University Press, 2018).

[26]Friedrich Nietzsche, *Twilight of the Idols and the AntiChrist,* trans. Thomas Common, Dover Philosophical Classics (New York: Dover, 2004), 13.

[27]In context, Hart was remarking on a Grateful Dead concert that he likened to an invocation. Mickey Hart, *Drumming at the Edge of Magic* (Petaluma, CA: Acid Test Productions, 1998), 212.

[28]Mark Helprin, *A Soldier of the Great War* (New York: Harcourt Brace, 1991), 263.

into art, above all in the music."[29] But also the fruit, which has been among the most original, moving and beautiful of any contribution to the arts. Perhaps this unlikely fruit is the reason some people do not know where to place the art of Black people. The remarkable African American poet and music critic Stanley L. Crouch (1945–2020) once quipped, "Troublesome person, that Negro—especially one with an aesthetic."[30] Obtaining a deeper knowledge of jazz will necessarily expose us to the unique contributions of African Americans. Duke Ellington, perhaps the most complete jazz artist ever, once remarked that "the foundation of the United States rests on the sweat of my people."[31] The music we call jazz cannot be divorced from the sorrows and joys of African Americans.

If this book accomplishes nothing else, it will have been worth the while if the reader becomes inspired to listen with open ears to this marvelous music. Or, if the reader needs no defense for the significance of jazz, perhaps he or she will have been exposed to a greater variety than previously acknowledged. If the book really succeeds, it will persuade the reader that the music cannot be properly understood without some familiarity with the Christian message. This does not mean one must be a theologian to grasp the message. But it will help to know the basics of creation, the fall into sin, and the redemption of all things by the grace of God. These basic tenets find their way into jazz, in the language of music, of course.

It is my conviction that if we are going to understand the deeper significance of jazz, including seminal works like Duke Ellington's "Take the A Train," Louis Armstrong's "What a Wonderful World," or John Coltrane's album *A Love Supreme*, then we need to attend to its relation to the gospel of Jesus Christ, which moves from the deep pain and sorrow of the crucifixion to the joy of the resurrection. By knowing the historical roots of jazz and by being better listeners, I believe we will hear something that is deeply embedded in jazz: a supreme love—the love of God.

---

[29]Kertin W. Shands and Giulia Grillo Mikrut, eds., *Living Language, Living Memory: Essays on the Works of Toni Morrison* (Flemingsberg: Södertörn University Press, 2014), 181.

[30]Stanley Crouch, "The Negro Aesthetic of Jazz," *Jazz Times* (October 2002).

[31]Cited in Harvey G. Cohen, *Duke Ellington's America* (Chicago: University of Chicago Press, 2010), 394.

PART I

HISTORICAL CONTEXT

A LONG WAY
FROM HOME

SLAVERY AND DIASPORA

*I am not ashamed of my grandparents for having
been slaves. I am only ashamed of myself
for having at one time been ashamed.*

RALPH ELLISON

If the jazz aesthetic moves us from deep misery to inextinguishable joy, we will need to explore the sources of that misery. In this and the next few chapters we want to describe some of the contours of the historical context of slavery and the way music emerged from that experience. Students and scholars of the history of slavery will no doubt find this account incomplete. But its essential delineations must be stated.

EXODUS

African American music was first produced by a people in diaspora.[1] The numbers are sobering and disheartening. Between 1525 and 1866, 12.5 million Africans were captured, enslaved, and shipped to the New

---

[1]See Samuel A. Floyd, Jr., with Melanie Zeck and Guthrie Ramsay, *The Transformation of Black Music: The Rhythms, the Songs, and the Ships of the African Diaspora* (New York: Oxford University Press, 2017).

World, including South America, the Caribbean Islands, and North America. Of those, 10.7 million survived the passage. Perhaps surprisingly, only 388,000 landed in North America.[2]

There is a most poignant monument in Ouidah, in the current Republic of Benin in West Africa, called *La Porte du Non-retour*, the "Door of No Return." Shaped like a giant gate, it was the last place slaves would cross before being dragged onto shipboard with cruel chains. Never again would they be able to see their loved ones or their homeland. This is one of four such places along the West Coast of Africa where the slaves were put onto the atrocious ships that carried them across the sea to the New World.

It is often forgotten that the continent of Africa had been a significant place for biblical religion well before the modern period. Of course, the people of Israel found a home in Egypt, through Joseph's enslavement, generations before they entered the Promised Land. We might also think of the Queen of Sheba and her entourage coming to sit at the feet of King Solomon (1 Kings 10:1-13). We should not forget that Jesus found refuge in Egypt along with Mary and Joseph before returning to Nazareth (Mt 2:13-23). We also may take note of people of African descent in the New Testament church, including the Ethiopian eunuch (Acts 8:26-40), the prophet Niger (Acts 13:1), and later the remarkable theologians among the fathers, including Tertullian (160–220) and Augustine (354–430). Even after the Arab conquests, there were strongholds of Christian faith in places such as Egypt, Algeria, and Tunisia. Yet by the time of modern slavery, Europeans had forgotten this heritage, allowing themselves to caricature Africans as "primitives" or "savages" lacking in civilization—despite the fact that Africa has always been part of the story of Christianity.

For that matter, it is crucial to remember that there has been a long and rich tradition of music-making in West Africa. It was impossible that

---

[2]In their remarkable work, authors David Eltis and David Richardson illustrate the hundreds of ways ships journeyed from the Old World to the New: David Eltis and David Richardson, *Atlas of the Transatlantic Slave Trade* (New Haven, CT: Yale University Press, 2015); Markus Rediker, *The Slave Ship: A Human History* (New York: Viking, 2007), 5; and Raymond L. Cohn, "Death of Slaves in the Middle Passage," *Journal of Economic History* 45, no. 3 (1985): 687.

some retentions of this history would not occur in the New World, despite attempts to cut slaves off from their roots. We do not know a great deal about the forms and practice of music in those countries from which slaves were taken, though a few accounts have come down from observers. We do know that music and dance accompanied every aspect of life, from work to warfare, to weddings and numerous other ceremonies. Olaudah Equiano, in his valuable chronicle of the life of slavery, tells us, "We are almost a nation of dancers, musicians and poets. Thus, every great event . . . is celebrated in public dances which are accompanied with songs and music suited to the occasion."[3]

SLAVERS REVENGING THEIR LOSSES.

Figure 1.1. Slaves captured in West Africa begin their long, sad journey

Slaves were captured in West Africa, sometimes the victims of bitter rivalries between African monarchs, often captured by corrupt European colonists and merchants. Many kidnappers raided tribes and traded human chattel for money, commodities, and other goods. The captives were marched in chains down to the coast and held in jails called barracoons. After sales negotiations, they were then forced on to ships which

[3]Olaudah Equiano, *The Interesting Narrative of the Life of Olaudah Equiano* (New York: Penguin Books, 2003), 34.

carried them to the Americas. Though it is true that sometimes slaves were captured by fellow Africans (exploitation being an equal opportunity disease), without the White man's drive to subjugate the Black person and turn him into a labor machine, modern slavery could not have occurred.

JES' WHERE TO GO I DID NOT KNOW

Not a great deal is known about the middle passage between Africa and the New World, but the conditions were certainly horrific.[4] Slaves were stuffed into the holds of galley ships that could contain several hundred detainees. Chained together, there was barely any room to move, and conditions were putrid.

Notable for our purposes is the slaver's assertion that the captives were kept "healthy" through song and dance.[5] In reality, they were forced into these dances and encouraged to smile, which often they did to avoid harassment. Women were particularly vulnerable to abuse from the slavers. The chronicler James Barbot affirmed that "the females being apart from the males and on the quarter deck and many of them young sprightly maidens, full of jollity and good humor, afford us an abundance of recreation."[6] One does not have to try very hard at reading between the lines. A more honest testimony is from the abolitionist Thomas Clarkson, who affirmed the captives were "compelled to dance by the cat" (the cat o' nine tails, a whip).[7]

---

[4]One of the most instructive studies is Maria Diedrich, Henry Louis Gates Jr., and Carl Pedersen, eds., *Black Imagination and the Middle Passage* (New York: Oxford University Press, 1999). A poignant account of slave mutinies is Eric Robert Taylor, *If We Must Die: Shipboard Insurrections in the Era of the Atlantic Slave Trade* (Baton Rouge: Louisiana State University Press, 2009). See also Marcus Rediker, *The Slave Ship: A Human History* (New York: Viking, 2007); Sowande' M. Mustakeem, *Slavery at Sea: Terror, Sex and Sickness in the Middle Passage* (Urbana: University of Illinois Press, 2016).

[5]Katrina Dyonne Thompson, *Ring Shout, Wheel About: The Racial Politics of Music and Dance in North American Slavery* (Urbana: University of Illinois Press, 2014), 54.

[6]From George Francis Dow, *Slave Ships and Slaving* (Baltimore, MD: Cornell Maritime Press, Tidewater, 1968), 50.

[7]Thomas Clarkson, *An Abstract of the Evidence Delivered Before a Selected Committee of The House of Commons in the years 1790 and 1791 on the Part of the Petitioners for the Abolition of the Slave Trade* (London: James Phillips & George Yard, 1791), 37.

One of the most poignant descriptions of the harrowing conditions on the middle passage is in Eric Robert Taylor's *If We Must Die*. Cruelty, torture, near-starvation, rape, and abuse made death for some preferable to life on these ships.[8] Revolts were attempted, though most failed. Some succeeded, however, giving testimony to the willingness of slaves to resist, even to the point of martyrdom.[9]

What kind of music was heard on the evil boats of the middle passage? A certain Dr. Claxton records that aboard the slave ship *The Young Hero*, "They sing, but not for their amusement. To stave off melancholy that often led to revolt or suicide, the captain ordered them to sing, and they sang songs of sorrow. Their sickness, fear of being beaten, their hunger, and the memory of their country, are the usual subjects."[10] A similar testimony comes from the ship surgeon Alexander Falconbridge: "Their music, upon these occasions, consists of a drum. The poor wretches are frequently compelled to sing also: but when they do, their songs are generally, as may naturally be expected, melancholy lamentations of their exile from their native land." And he adds, "Such were the sad origins of the Negro rhythms which have since conquered the Western world."[11] Here we see the roots of the misery, sorrow, and pain that would come to be an indelible aspect of jazz. And we see evidence of the fact that music is not always about that which pleases or brings joy.

Black drama specialist Geneviève Fabre makes the interesting point that some of the dances on shipboard developed into standard rituals practiced once the slaves were on dry land. The limbo, for example, still performed in the Caribbean, is a dance wherein the actors recall their shackles, moving close to the ground, under an increasingly lowered bar,

---

[8] Taylor, *If We Must Die*, 23-39.

[9] Taylor, *If We Must Die*, 119-63. The book's title is a quote from a poem by Jamaican poet Claude McKay, which has these lines: "If we must die, let it not be like hogs hunted and penned in an inglorious spot . . . pressed to the wall, dying, but fighting back!" See also Claude McKay, *Harlem Shadows: The Poems of Claude McKay* (New York: Angelico, 2021), 47.

[10] From Daniel P. Mannix with Malcolm Cowley, *Black Cargoes: A History of the Atlantic Slave Trade, 1518-1865* (New York: Viking, 1962), 114.

[11] James Pope-Hennessy, *Sins of the Fathers: A Study of the Atlantic Slave Trade* (New York: Knopf, 1968), 4.

then emerge on the other side. This is a kind of "dance of life" in which "the leap to freedom is dramatized, visualized and narrated."[12]

Some of the most revealing, if heartbreaking, accounts show how Black people in captivity were conveniently viewed as commodities with customs supposedly different from European standards of decency. Almost all of them are written by White or European slavers, so they are certainly not objective, and yet still the horrors are patent. Various remedies were sought to preserve life, since the cargo represented huge profits. One method was called "jumping," which held that exercise kept bodies fit. This was nothing if not humiliating. The slaver Theodore Canot described a visit to a so-called slave factory in which he was entertained by a "harem" of half-naked women dancing in a "semi-savage" manner. His language makes it clear that he regarded these dancers as seductresses whose lascivious gestures showed them to be objects for the lusts of European men rather than human beings with any dignity.[13]

One early chronicler, Leo Africanus, comments that African people "addict themselves to nought else but delights and pleasure, feasting often and singing lascivious songs," which led them to "unlawful and filthie lust."[14] Africanus, who was himself African, was at the service of the Roman Catholic Church and thought that slavery was a means to bringing Africans to faith, which was a typical view held by a slave-keeper who boasted that he had been an instrument for the salvation of more souls than "all the missionaries in Africa."[15]

---

[12]Geneviève Fabre, "The Slave Ship Dance," in Diedrich, Gates, and Pederson, *Black Imagination and the Middle Passage*, 42.

[13]Theodore Canot, *Adventures of an African Slaver: Being a True Account of Captain Theodore Canot, Trader in Gold, Ivory and Slaves on the Coast of Guinea* (New York: Boni, 1928), 70.

[14]Leo Africanus, *The History and Description of Africa and of the Notable Things Contained Therein*, trans. John Pory, ed. Robert Brown (New York: Cambridge University Press, 2010), 2:464. The author attributes much of this disturbing behavior to gluttony. Translator John Pory seems to have embellished the text for consumption by European readers. An imaginative first-person retelling of Africanus's adventures is by Amin Maalouf, *Leo Africanus*, trans. Peter Sluggett (Chicago: New Amsterdam, 1998).

[15]Quoted in T. J. Bowen, *Adventures and Missionary Labours in Several Countries in the Interior of Africa from 1849 to 1846*, 2nd ed. (Boston: Routledge, 1968), 18. In their powerful book, Jason Reynolds and Ibram X. Kendi describe the sadly common argument by

DUST, DUST AND ASHES
FLY OVER MY GRAVE[16]

Of course, the passage across the ocean was just the beginning of the suffering of slaves. Once ashore, slaves consistently felt the dehumanizing reality of their condition. This was perhaps most poignantly and heartbreakingly demonstrated at the auction block. Consider just one example: at a racecourse near Savannah, Georgia, a large estate was broken up in 1859. For weeks, the auction was advertised. There were 436 slaves to be sold, including men, women, children, and infants. The slaves were put into horse stalls and were on display for days before the bidding. Although families were not supposed to be separated, separations did occur. The justification for avoiding split-ups was not moral principle but business practice, because when separated from their families, slaves were more discouraged and thus less productive. The auction was big, perhaps the largest ever, and it received such attention that Horace Greeley, editor of the influential *Herald Tribune*, sent a reporter to cover the event. As Greeley was a fierce abolitionist, he had hoped to show the world what a barbaric scene would unfold. During the inspection period, buyers were allowed to pry open the slaves' mouths to see if they had good teeth, to walk them up and down like dogs, and other humiliations. Some of the slaves took the degradation with a smile, hoping for masters who might treat them better.

Although this particular auction was one of the largest recorded, it was typical of the way such transactions occurred. The tragic event of the auction block became known to Black people as the "Weeping Time," the name given by the people who would never see their former home again and would spend their lives weeping over the forced migration to other

---

pro-slavery advocates that enslavement led to Christian conversion. In an ironic twist, Africanus wrote about his own people as "savages," who could be led to Jesus through their captivity. Reynolds and Kendi name him the first known African racist: Jason Reynolds and Ibram X. Kendi, *Stamped: Racism, Antiracism and You* (New York: Little Brown, 2020), 8.

[16]"And the Lord Shall Bear My Spirit Home" is the resolution. The spiritual exhibits the heart of our thesis: deep misery to inextinguishable joy. See Edith Armstrong Talbot, "True Religion in Southern Hymns, III," *The Southern Workman* 51, no. 7 (1922): 335.

places and separation from their own families.[17] Here is how one former slave, Jennie Hill, described the drama of the auction block:

> Some people think that slaves had no feeling—that they bore their children as animals bear their young and that there was no heartbreak when the children were torn from their parents or the mother taken from her brood to toil for a master in another state. But that isn't so. They sold one of Mother's children once, and when she take on and cry about it, the Master would say, "Stop that sniffing there if you don't want to get a whipping." She would grieve and cry at night about it.[18]

One commonly held belief was that certain slavers purchased slaves in order to save them from greater harm. Admiral Sir Charles Elliott recounts the claim of one Methodist minister who said he purchased slaves under the concept of the "mercy to the slave purchase." This cleric claimed that he purchased ten thousand dollars' worth of slaves in order to save them from a worse fate. Elliott is quick to condemn this as hypocrisy because it allowed the slave owner to perpetuate an evil tradition under the cover of "mercy."[19]

Slaves were not allowed to marry legally until 1830 in the North and not until after the Civil War in the rest of the country. It was often the case that a Black male slave was owned by one master and the mother of his children by another. Ceremonies known as "jumping the broom" were concocted to simulate weddings. The long-term effects of breaking families apart have been documented. Daniel Patrick Moynihan, working for the Office of Policy Planning in the Labor department under Lyndon

---

[17]"Slave Auction, 1859," *Eyewitness to History*, www.eyewitnesstohistory.com/slaveauction.htm.

[18]Michael Tadman, *Speculators and Slaves: Masters, Traders and Slaves in the Old South* (Madison: University of Wisconsin Press, 1989), 219-20. Tadman estimates that at least one out of every five marriages were terminated because the spouses were sold to two different slaveholders. One of every two children under the age of fourteen was torn away from home.

[19]Charles Elliott, *The Sinfulness of American Slavery* (Cincinnati: L. Swormstedt & J. H. Power, 1850), 2:294.

Johnson, wrote a report in 1965 called "The Negro Family: The Case for National Action," which analyzed the sources of urban poverty and unrest. Drawing on the work of African American sociologist E. Franklin Frazer, he concluded that its roots could be found in slavery. The report pointed to "a racist virus in the American bloodstream" that had resulted in three centuries of "unimaginable mistreatment" that continued to plague Black communities.[20]

How could the music that grew out of the realities of the enslavement of Black people, forced migration, rape, husbands and wives being separated, and children being ripped from their families not reflect this suffering and pain? If, as I will argue, jazz is the story of deep misery that leads to inextinguishable joy, then we cannot ignore the sources of sorrow that are found at the root of this music, from spirituals to blues to jazz.

One of the spirituals, or "sorrow songs" as W. E. B. Du Bois called them, that reflects the depths of this suffering is "Sometimes I feel like a motherless child":

Sometimes I feel like a motherless child

Sometimes I feel like a motherless child

Sometimes I feel like a motherless child

A long way from home, a long way from home

Sometimes I feel like I'm almost done

Sometimes I feel like I'm almost done

Sometimes I feel like I'm almost done

And a long, long way from home, a long way from home

True believer

---

[20]See Heather Andrea Williams, "How Slavery Affected African American Families," *Freedom's Story: Teaching African American Literature and History*, http://nationalhumanities center.org/tserve/freedom/1609-1865/essays/aafamilies.htm.

True believer

A long, long way from home

A long, long way from home.[21]

---

[21]There are many versions of this classic; among the most haunting is by Bessie Griffin. See
"Bessie Griffin—Sometimes I Feel Like A Motherless Child," YouTube video, 5:22, posted
by "Princebbl," December 22, 2008, www.youtube.com/watch?v=2NDwW8onaoA.

2

PATERNALISM

JUSTIFYING NARRATIVES

Swaying to and fro on his rickety stool
He played that sad raggy tune like a musical fool
Sweet Blues!

LANGSTON HUGHES

T he deep misery found in jazz is rooted in the harrowing experience of slavery. Most history books contain a sentiment that is something like this: America was born as a great experiment in freedom. But two great contradictions to this quest were the treatment of Africans and Native Americans. Today, we rightly view such assessments of American history as hopelessly shallow and limited.

Slavery took place within the larger context of colonialism. The scholar Vincent Brown compares the Atlantic slave trade to a war. In his extensive study of slavery and its causes on Jamaica Island, focusing on the most notorious revolt in the colony's history, he highlights the metaphor of war. For this he takes his cue from the endeavors of Olaudah Equiano, a key player in the abolition movement that led Great Britain to forbid the slave trade and slavery itself. Indeed, Equiano characterized slavery as "a state of war."[1] "The seeds of insurrection," he writes, "surely germinated in

---

[1]Vincent Brown, *Tacky's Revolt: The Story of an Atlantic Slave War* (Cambridge, MA: Belknap, 2020), 73.

Africa, but they sprouted in the fertile soil of American slavery's brutal violence. And they flowered in the light of imperial warfare, as Britain vied with France for superiority in the North Atlantic."[2]

RACE AND JUSTIFICATIONS

What was the background for such a war? The ostensible purpose for slavery was cheap labor. That is only part of the story, however. Slaves were viewed as legal property; they were bought and sold as chattel. Such an inhuman practice demanded some kind of justification. Historian Niall Ferguson notes that the philosophical justification for slavery in the Carolinas drew strongly from John Locke's view that property is the most fundamental of human rights. "Carolina, Locke declared, shall have absolute power and authority over his negro slaves, of what opinion or religion soever."[3] Ferguson contrasts North American with South American slavery, arguing that the Spanish approach that characterized South America centered on wealth and authoritarianism, which made it easier to break with the system than in the North, which viewed slaves as a property right, whose effects still bedevil us.[4]

Defenders of slavery often claimed that it was practiced, and not necessarily condemned, in biblical times. Certainly, a form of it was practiced in Old Testament times. This precedent, however, was often misused to argue that there was no summary condemnation of the practice in Scripture. Most of these defenders thought that modern slavery had become excessive, but not altogether immoral. Jochem Douma, who taught ethics at Kampen, disagreed, arguing that slavery is a form of stealing, which of course *is* specifically forbidden in the Bible. His book on the Ten Commandments treats the subject under the Eighth Commandment ("You shall not steal") as a form of kidnapping, noting that the inclusion of kidnappers in the list in 1 Timothy 1:10 alongside other truly

---

[2]Brown, *Tacky's Revolt*, 85. Territorial and political control were as much at stake in slavery (and insurrection) as cheap labor.
[3]Niall Ferguson, *Civilization: The West and the Rest* (New York: Penguin Books, 2011), 135.
[4]Ferguson, *Civilization*, 138.

heinous sins should not surprise us.[5] He points out that the better translation of the Greek is "man-stealing" or "slave-trading," and he further
reminds us that buying or selling a human being is a crime punishable by
death in the Old Testament (Ex 21:16). He also points out that there was
legitimate forced servitude in the Old Testament that had nothing to do
with modern slavery. Indeed, provisions were made for freeing slaves as
soon as possible, with an appeal to Israel not to forget their own enslavement in Egypt. We might ask, then, why did it take Americans so
long to see the sin of slavery and react against it?

In my view, the fundamental characteristic of the culture in which
the dominant classes practiced the unspeakable cruelty of slavery is
paternalism. Or, as it could also be put, as colonization of the soul. This,
along with the different attempts to defend slavery, is at the heart of a
culture that could defend such abhorrent practices. As a justification
for this ideology, paternalism argues that the enslaved need, and indeed
benefit from, the oversight of the slaveowner, while at the same time
denying the fundamental dignity of human beings created in the image
of God. W. E. B. Du Bois wrote of the "disastrous effects" of a system
whereby "a man could be, under the law, the actual master of the mind
and body of human beings."[6] In underscoring paternalism, Du Bois was
prescient of what later scholars would elucidate. He saw segregation as
a matter of class, rather than race, and he argued strongly that discrimination had no bearing on biology. Paternalism was a way to maintain
privilege. Not without gratitude, Du Bois saw even some of the better
conceived charities and educational endeavors in the North as well as
the South as limited in scope. Rarely were they designed to position
Black people for direct competitions with Whites for self-directed
social positions. This is also the assessment of historian Eugene
Genovese, who likens the slaves' relationship to the master to the

---

[5]Jochem Douma, *The Ten Commandments: Manual for the Christian Life*, trans. Nelson D.
Kloosterman (Phillipsburg, NJ: P&R, 1996), 285-89.
[6]W. E. B. Du Bois, *Black Reconstruction in America, 1860–1880* (New York: Free Press,
1935), 52.

godfather figure, "who simultaneously protects and abuses, nourishes and punishes."[7]

A common rationalization for paternalism, used to placate White consciences, was to consider Black people as less than fully human. Indeed, they were considered property rather than persons. Furthermore, many White owners convinced themselves that "Negroes" were closer to animals, following base instincts, than to civilized people. There is considerable cruel irony here, in that when slaves were accused of breaking a law, they were suddenly considered to be humans who were guilty under the law.

How could such a view be justified? Social justice activist Bryan Stevenson rightly points to the underlying narrative of white supremacy employed to explain slavery: "I actually think the great evil of American slavery wasn't simply the involuntary servitude and forced labor. The true evil of American slavery was the narrative we created to justify it. They made up this ideology of white supremacy that cannot be reconciled with our Constitution, that cannot be reconciled with a commitment to fair and just treatment."[8] Recent discussions of race rightly see racism as involving *systemic* levels of prejudice that reflect this same sentiment.[9]

What is unutterably sad and inexcusable is that the cruel paternalism of slavery was often sanitized in Christian language. The Portuguese claimed a number of territories on the African continent "in the name of God, the pope, and the king." In travel narratives from that era, we regularly find biased characterizations of Black people in order to justify purging them of paganism, defending their enslavement, and then leading them to the Christian faith. The fact that some Black slaves became

---

[7]Eugene D. Genovese, *Roll, Jordan, Roll: The World the Slaves Made* (New York: Vintage, 1976), 120.

[8]Bryan Stevenson, "Bryan Stevenson Explains How It Feels to Grow Up Black amid Confederate Monuments," by Ezra Klein, *Vox*, May 24, 2017, www.vox.com/2017/5/24/15675606 /bryan-stevenson-confederacy-monuments-slavery-ezra-klein, quoted in Henry Louis Gates Jr., *Stony the Road: Reconstruction, White Supremacy, and the Rise of Jim Crow* (New York: Penguin Books, 2019), 1.

[9]See Jemar Tisby, *The Color of Compromise: The Truth About the American Church's Complicity in Racism* (Grand Rapids: Zondervan, 2020); Ibram X. Kendi, *How to Be an Antiracist* (New York: One World, 2019).

Christian and that the music that grew out of these tragic circumstances resonates with the Christian message in no way excuses or justifies such mistreatment of bearers of the divine image.

In this light, I am reminded of the following spiritual:

Dark and thorny is de pathway

Where de pilgrim makes his ways

But beyond dis vale of sorrow

Lie de fields of endless days.[10]

THE HAPPY, MUSICALLY GIFTED SLAVE?

Another narrative that was developed in order to somehow justify, or at least mollify, the reality of slavery was the fable of the "happy Negro." When the slave trade was finally coming under scrutiny in Great Britain, slavers took pains to justify it by testifying that their captives were treated fairly and were even quite naturally cheerful in their dispositions. We have testimonies before the British Parliament of witnesses such as the Liverpool slaver Robert Norris. Norris is cited by William Wilberforce, the famous reformer whose arguments persuaded a reluctant Parliament to end slavery, as having misled the Parliament by testifying that slaves were comfortable, even happy to leave their homelands.

To be sure, there is often in the best of the music of Black people a degree of mirth, but this should never be confused with deep joy. For example, footage of Louis Armstrong's jazz demonstrates a celebration of sorts, but it is not the same as the faux-mirth encouraged by ship captains and later slave drivers.[11] Armstrong himself has been subject to this sort of caricature in this matter. He nearly always displayed a cheerful demeanor

---

[10]Occasionally in quotes from various songs and texts, I have kept the vernacular—for example, "Dark and thorny is de pathway" instead of "the" pathway. By doing this, I intend to respect the original without imposing the exigencies of modern English.

[11]See, for example, his performance of "Dinah" from 1933: "Louis Armstrong 'Dinah' 1933," YouTube video, 2:52, from a performance in Copenhagen, posted by "harryoakley," March 3, 2009, www.youtube.com/watch?v=BhVdLd43bDI.

and smiled and chuckled in his performances. His exuberance even became an embarrassment to fellow Black musicians in his later years. For example, his lifetime ambition to become the "King of the Zulus" in New Orleans's Mardi Gras parade was considered a vestige "of the minstrel-show, Sambo-type Negro."[12] Dizzy Gillespie, the great bebop trumpeter, remarked several times that Armstrong displayed "Uncle Tom-like subservience," and called him a "plantation character." But Armstrong felt very strongly about race issues, and he was sharply critical of policies involving segregation and racist injustice. His performance jubilation was not incompatible with these feelings. To his credit, Dizzy later took back his jibes and recognized that Armstrong had a unique way of dealing with racism.[13]

Another central myth developed to justify the kind of racial typecasting that could lead to excusing slavery was the widely held conviction that Africans were somehow more naturally gifted in music and dance than Whites. As people, Africans are in fact no more and no less gifted in the musical arts than any other people. It is also true that for cultural reasons, music and dance may have a more prominent role among Africans than among other groups. Deprived of so much else in slavery, these skills somehow survived and expressed the pain and misery of such conditions. Thomas Jefferson, himself a slave owner, wrote: "In music they are more generally gifted than the whites with accurate ears for tune and time." He added some odd reflections: "Whether they will be equal to the composition of a more extensive run of melody, or of complicated harmony, is yet to be proved." And then the strange statement: "Misery is often the parent of the most affecting touches in poetry.—Among the blacks is misery enough, God knows, but no poetry."[14] He seems to have ignored (or was ignorant of) the beauty of spirituals, or the talents of a number of poets such as Phillis Wheatley, or even Benjamin Banneker (1731–1806), a poet and city planner who corresponded with him about

---

[12]Terry Teachout, *Pops: A Life of Louis Armstrong* (Boston: Houghton Mifflin Harcourt, 2009), 324.

[13]Teachout, *Pops*, 336. Tellingly, Dizzy also admitted that he had his own way of "Tomming."

[14]Thomas Jefferson, *Notes on the State of Virginia*, Queries 14 & 18, http://press-pubs .uchicago.edu/founders/documents/v1ch15s28.html.

slavery.[15] But expressions of musical gifts, which were rife with evidence of suffering, could not be used to justify the "happy" existence of slaves.

SLAVES AND NATIVE AMERICANS

"Knowledge makes a man unfit to be a slave." This quote from Frederick Douglass gives a partial reason for the absurdity of slavery. Christians in the biblical tradition would appeal to the image of God but then fail to connect this doctrine to a policy of abolition. Slavery was not simply a stain on an otherwise enlightened Western civilization. It was a sinister force endemic to the colonialism of the European powers. Paternalism is a crucial part of the social structure that promoted such aggressive oppression. Besides the brutality of it, the structure put in place was meant to colonize the soul.

Historian Greg Grandin has argued that entitlement has been characteristic not only of prejudice against Black people but against other minority peoples, particularly Native Americans.[16] Grandin, following Martin Luther King Jr., traces the history of Manifest Destiny. In his book *Why We Can't Wait*, King made the controversial statement that "our nation was founded on genocide." The rest of the sentence reads, "when it embraced the doctrine that the original American, the Indian, was an inferior race."[17]

Genocide is a serious charge. And yet it is the case that westward expansion is related to the atrocities of slavery. Among other things, this expansion required laborers to reap its benefits. But such expansion was much more than just finding the means to sustain economic growth; it was the growing belief that moving west meant moving toward hope and freedom, at least for some. In his study *How Does America Hear the Gospel?*, theologian William Dyrness argues that the vast expanses of western

---

[15]Jeffrey Einboden sets things straight in *Jefferson's Muslim Fugitives: The Lost Story of Enslaved Africans, Their Arabic Letters, and an American President* (New York: Oxford University Press, 2020).

[16]Greg Grandin, *The End of the Myth* (New York: Henry Holt, 2020). See also Richard Twiss, *Rescuing the Gospel from the Cowboys: A Native American Expression of the Jesus Way* (Downers Grove, IL: IVP Academic, 2015).

[17]Martin Luther King Jr., *Why We Can't Wait* (New York: Signet, 2000).

America were mythologized as virgin territories to be claimed for numerous ambitions.[18] For some it was a geography of hope. Religious groups such as the Mormons sought to escape the confines of Eastern religious prejudices and arrive at a new Jerusalem. The discovery of gold triggered a great rush west, often full of conflict and corruption. The Lewis and Clark expedition sought to establish better trade with Native Americans as well as to find a waterway to the Pacific. Yet it is undeniable that the move westward often entailed outright subjugation.[19] Maps have been found that highlight counties with slaves, Amerindians, and their numbers, presumably to show as yet unconquered places. Manifest Destiny often entailed a justification for the eradication, or at least the marginalization, of large populations of Native Americans. There were appeasements, treaties, and negotiations for hunting grounds, but many of those were later ignored or broken. Yet we must not romanticize any group. Some tribes were capable of enormous cruelty. The idea of the "noble savage" is being tempered with more factual accounts which include violence and oppression.[20] Even so, the story is tragic, and its justifying narratives and inexcusable practices parallel in many ways the treatment of enslaved Black people.

While in no way justifying such treatment, there is a kind of silver lining in the music world. It happens that there are scores of Native Americans who have become prominent jazz musicians. Consider the music of Matthew Parrish,[21] Charles Mingus, Doc Cheatham, Jimmy Blanton, Lionel Hampton, and Charlie Parker.[22] Like the Black musicians we have described, these artists subvert the system of oppression by playing superbly. Is there a distinctive Native American style? Artie Shaw played *Indian Love Call*, featuring tom-tom-like rhythms, a wistful melody, and

[18]William A. Dyrness, *How Does America Hear the Gospel?* (Grand Rapids: Eerdmans, 1990).

[19]The story is told, depressingly, by Greg Grandin, *The End of the Myth: From Frontier to Border Wall in the Mind of America* (New York: Metropolitan Books, 2019).

[20]Matthew Jennings, "Terrorism in North America from the Colonial Period to John Brown," in *The Routledge History of Terrorism*, ed. Randall D. Law (New York: Routledge, 2015), 78.

[21]"Biography," on Matthew Parrish's official website, www.matthewparrish.org/bio/.

[22]See Bill Sullivan, "Native Americans in Jazz—Present and Past," Hartford Jazz Society, July 21, 2017, https://hartfordjazzsociety.com/2017/07/21/native-americans-in-jazz-present -and-past/.

some stereotypical call-and-response choruses.[23] Jimmy Pepper's *Pow Wow* is more infused with Native American words and sounds.[24]

Recently, activist Nikole Hannah-Jones has directed a serious initiative, the 1619 Project, whose mission is to reframe America's history by dating the beginning of America not to 1776 and the American Revolution, but to 1619, when the first slave ship landed on these shores. She has provocatively argued that the American Revolution was intended to protect the institution of slavery. Whether one agrees with her project or not, it is undeniable that America's history has been profoundly shaped by the horrific treatment of groups including Black people and Native Americans. Such dehumanizing treatment inevitably shaped the musical expressions found in jazz. Consider the powerful spiritual "Nobody Knows":

Nobody knows the trouble I've seen

Nobody knows but Jesus

Nobody knows the trouble I've seen

Glory, Hallelujah

Sometimes I'm up, sometimes

I'm down, oh, yes Lord

Sometimes I'm almost

To the ground, oh yes, Lord

Nobody knows the trouble I've seen

Nobody knows but Jesus

Anybody knows the trouble I've seen

Glory, Hallelujah.

---

[23]"Artie Shaw - Indian love call," YouTube video, 3:11, from Artie Shaw's *99 Hits* album, posted by "OnlyJazzHQ," February 5, 2013, www.youtube.com/watch?v=nr5hSsNpvig.

[24]"Jim Pepper Witchitai-to," YouTube video, 8:09, from Jim Pepper's *Pepper's Pow Wow* (1971) album, posted by "grizzrocks," August 31, 2008, www.youtube.com/watch?v=S2YeEUlyhQw.

3

BONDAGE
AND BEAUTY

LIFE AND MUSIC
DURING SLAVERY

Now I've been free, I know what a dreadful condition

slavery is. I have seen hundreds of escaped slaves,

but I never saw one who was willing to go back and be a slave.

HARRIET TUBMAN

We will never know the whole story of slave life or the depths of the hardships suffered, but we do have a number of different kinds of records, and an increasing number of narratives are seeing the light of day. Reading the scores of chronicles by slaves or former slaves can be very sobering, at times sickening. My own theology acknowledges the reality of human depravity. But this doctrine did not prepare me for confronting the accounts of the cruelty and systematic malice endured by slaves from their masters and even more often from the foreman or overseer.

The writings of Frederick Douglass are among the clearest and most honest ever penned on this subject, despite attempts by editors to tone down his prose. It is nearly impossible for any sensitive person to get through these lines without revulsion. Douglass gives accounts of whipping a disabled woman with a heavy cow skin to the brink of death. He describes a Captain Auld, who prior to his conversion "relied upon his own depravity to shield and sustain him in his savage barbarity; but after his conversion, he found religious sanction and support for his slaveholding cruelty."[1] He described an owner named Mr. Covey, who worked the slaves until eleven or twelve at night, whipping them at least once a week so they could not run away.[2] Such accounts provide essential firsthand accounts of the dehumanizing conditions of slavery. Facts are stubborn and not easily set aside, and these facts need to be heard.

GORDON UNDER MEDICAL INSPECTION.

Figure 3.1. "Gordon Under Medical Inspection": A photograph of a formerly enslaved man identified only as Private Gordon evidences the cruelty of slavery.

[1]Frederick Douglass, *Narrative of the Life of Frederick Douglass, an American Slave* (New York: Simon & Brown, 2013), 53.
[2]Douglass, *Narrative*, 238-49.

I COULDN'T HEAR NOBODY PRAY[3]

Although they were made to work in squalid conditions, the labor of the slaves was not restricted to the cotton fields or tobacco plantations. A distinction was made between house slaves and field slaves. House slaves were used as nannies, waiters, cooks, or accountants, whereas field slaves were used for more menial labor. This distinction was based in part on skin color and social class.[4] Certainly, discipline was harsh for both types, and in both cases there was punishment for not being productive enough, and women were vulnerable to sexual exploitation. Malcolm X sharply denounced the house slave as being "seasoned" in a way the field slave was not. In Malcolm's view this led to the domestication of the house slave, which authorized him to manage the field slave and keep him passive.[5] In that regard, the romanticized portrait of Hattie in *Gone with the Wind* is rightly deemed unacceptable today. The same is true for many older films in which Black servants are represented.

Even if the house slaves were given a few more privileges, however, life was anything but easy for them. Living in such close proximity, the house slaves were more likely to develop relationships with their owners. Often Black children played together with White children. Some developed a bond with their White mistress, just as Whites would become attached to the Black nannies, who were sometimes entrusted with the religious training of White children. But make no mistake; slavery was a harsh, cruel, and forbidding condition for all slaves. The reality was that a slave was the property of the head of the house, no matter what appearances may have been.

---

[3]It's a bit stylized, but Leontyne Price captures the feeling of solitude in her version of the song: "Leontyne Price: I Couldn't Hear Nobody Pray," YouTube video, 3:59, posted by "will-workforwages," February 17, 2013, www.youtube.com/watch?v=EnGsq0WET1A; a moving a cappella Black ensemble, *Choir Boy*, does it a bit differently: "Choir Boy Music Video: I Couldn't Hear Nobody Pray," YouTube video, 0:53, posted by "Manhattan Theater Club," December 11, 2018, www.youtube.com/watch?v=3DPNJsvi8WQ.

[4]"Recollection of Thirty Years Ago," quoted in Eugene D. Genovese, *Roll, Jordan, Roll: The World the Slaves Made* (New York: Vintage Books, 1976), 327, 734n1.

[5]From a speech given at the University of Michigan in East Lansing, January 23, 1963. See Vincent W. Lloyd, *Religion of the Field Negro* (New York: Fordham University Press, 2018), 1n1.

It may come as a surprise for some to discover that three-fourths of Southern White people did not own slaves, and that, for the most part, those who did kept only relatively few. Whites who did not own slaves were usually farmers, though they often aspired to own slaves as a symbol of social status. In any case, whether explicitly or implicitly, Southern White people condoned the institution of slavery.[6]

BEAUTY FROM ASHES

One of my friends today lives on his family's plantation. His home was built by slaves, and it was beautifully built. After emancipation, the freed slaves continued to live nearby, and today relations between the two communities of Black and White residents is relatively good. How might we account for such bright spots amid such tragedy and degradation? Is it possible to find beauty in the midst of bondage?

Were some slaveowners kinder than others? Yes. Did some Black freedmen fight alongside Union soldiers?[7] Yes. Yet the truth remains that slavery is founded on a dehumanizing ideology and that the colonization of the soul is among the greatest criminalities in human history. My friend is a Christian who does not believe slavery could ever have been justified, but he is certain that relations are relatively good today because his family treated the slaves humanely. But facts are stubborn, and the fact is that previous generations of his family owned other human beings. Relatively good relations today, from his viewpoint, do not justify the fact that slavery entailed the sinful ownership of humans made in the image of God.

Is it possible that music, too, was a bright spot in the midst of bondage? Might jazz, the roots of which were born in the crucible of slavery, contain elements of beauty? There have been other examples of such music created amid suffering. One psalm of lament, written in the

---

[6] See *Africans in America: Resource Bank, Conditions of Antebellum Slavery*, "Judgment Day," Part 4, www.pbs.org/wgbh/aia/part4/4p2956.html.
[7] Eugene Genovese, *Roll, Jordan, Roll: The World the Slaves Made* (New York: Vintage Books, 1976), 149-58.

context of the Babylonian captivity and exile, asks how a native song can be sung in captivity:

> By the waters of Babylon,
>
> there we sat down and wept,
>
> when we remembered Zion.
>
> On the willows there
>
> we hung up our lyres.
>
> For there our captors
>
> required of us songs,
>
> and our tormentors, mirth, saying,
>
> "Sing us one of the songs of Zion!"
>
> How shall we sing the LORD's song
>
> in a foreign land?
>
> If I forget you, O Jerusalem,
>
> let my right hand forget its skill!
>
> Let my tongue stick to the roof of my mouth,
>
> if I do not remember you,
>
> if I do not set Jerusalem
>
> above my highest joy! (Ps 137:1-6)

The nineteenth-century English preacher Charles Spurgeon commented on these lines: "Better be dumb than be forced to please an enemy with forced song."[8]

Likewise, victims of the Shoah in Nazi Germany produced heart-rending music. Such music-making might be a form for escape. But it was

---

[8]Charles Spurgeon, *The Treasury of David*, vol. 6, *Psalms 126–150* (Grand Rapids, MI: Zondervan, 1957), 268.

also a way to assert one's humanity amid an oppression bent on destroying it.[9] One of the most memorable incarceration pieces is by the extraordinary modern French composer Olivier Messiaen. His *Quartet for the End of Time*, based on the book of Revelation, was performed January 15, 1941, in the German prison camp, Stalag VIIIA.[10] It was performed outdoors in the rain before four hundred prisoners and guards. Later, Messiaen would say, "Never was I listened to with such rapt attention and comprehension."[11]

The music articulated by oppressed Black people during their lives as slaves possessed several notable characteristics. First, its emergence even amid such tragic circumstances testifies to the fact that music-making, and artistic creativity more broadly, is a fundamental human trait. In the biblical account, the first practitioners of culture-making included both vocal and instrumental music (Gen 4:21). What looks at first blush like a passing statement is, in fact, one of the building blocks for the human calling to make culture. Making music is thus on a level with city dwelling, agriculture, animal husbandry, and iron work (Gen 4:17-22).[12] Perhaps surprisingly, many Black slaves learned European music to play for balls and local ceremonies and became skilled at the fiddle, the French horn, and other instruments used for social events. In fact, it is quite possible that the baroque feeling of early New Orleans bands may have come from the style of playing in these European dances. But much of the music that developed in slavery had little relation to European dances. The "field call"

---

[9]See "Music of the Holocaust," United States Holocaust Memorial Museum, accessed December 30, 2021, www.ushmm.org/collections/the-museums-collections/collections-highlights/music-of-the-holocaust-highlights-from-the-collection/music-of-the-holocaust.

[10]For example, see "Digital Premiere—Quartet for the End of Time MetLiveArts," YouTube video, 47:42, posted by "The Met," April 20, 2021, www.youtube.com/watch?v=e2hbwINj7dE. A masterful study of this unique composition and its circumstances is Rebecca Rischin, *For the End of Time: A Study of the Messaien Quartet* (Ithaca, NY: Cornell University Press, 2006).

[11]Joseph Stevenson, *All Music Guide to Classical Music: The Definitive Guide to Classical Music* (Ann Arbor, MI: All Media Guide, 2005), 843.

[12]For a more developed argument on the foundations for music in human life, see my *Taking Note of Music* (London: SPCK, 1986). See also William Edgar, *Created and Creating: A Biblical Theology of Culture* (Downers Grove, IL: IVP Academic, 2016).

or "field holler" was music to work by, but these songs often carried coded messages of resistance.[13] Meanwhile, its parallel, the "complaint call" is a heartbreaking song of lament, which became the origin of the blues. Black music reflected all of the complexities, trauma, suffering, and—yes—joys of Black life.

A second trait, which we have already pointed to, is the element of sorrow that inevitably pervades this music as the direct result of enslavement and cruel treatment. It is the music of the motherless child. Music was never entirely absent from enslaved Africans, not because Black people are more naturally musical than others, but because human beings are inherently musical, and music was one of the few outlets for an enslaved people. How could this music not reveal the suffering of Black people?

They loudly talk of Christ's reward,

And bind his image with a cord,

And scold, and swing the lash abhorred,

And sell their brother in the Lord

To handcuffed heavenly union.[14]

But a third trait of the music articulated during slavery is its affirmation of survival and life. It stands like an unbroken mast in the storm, a protest-with-joy in the midst of sorrow and death. Such music of survival is not simply in contrast to the pervasive oppression of the surrounding culture, but in part dependent on it. Ethnomusicologist Ronald Radano reminds us that Black music is not only about separation but, strangely, about integration.[15] As one reviewer put it, "For well over a hundred years, black

---

[13]For two examples, see "Belton Sutherland's field hollar (1978)," YouTube video, 0:52, posted by "Alan Lomax Archive," May 14, 2012, www.youtube.com/watch?v=1CPJwt14d5E; and "Arwhoolie (Cornfield Hollar)," YouTube video, 0:54, posted by "MG Team 8 The Team," March 10, 2014, www.youtube.com/watch?v=ZPrZ-YsD6sc.

[14]Douglass, Narrative, 123.

[15]See Ronald Radano, Lying Up a Nation: Race and Black Music (Chicago: University of Chicago Press, 2003).

music has been held up as a symbol of the grandeur and distinctiveness of the nation, bringing into discernible sonic form all that which unites and divides us."[16] As in almost every culture, the songs emerging from the Black experience punctuated all of life, celebrating events, expressing emotions, recalling history, bringing people together. This affirmation of survival, this protest-with-joy is found in the music created by enslaved Black people, and it is the true posture of jazz music at its best. As we will see, joy is fundamentally different from happiness. Happiness does not reflect the human experience that has been hammered out on the anvil of suffering. Only a deeper joy can do that.

For a musical comparison, consider how much of contemporary Christian music—which is mostly White—expresses a *happiness* in contrast to the *joyfulness* of Black music, particularly spirituals. For example, compare the worship song "Calvary" by Hillsong Worship to Maurette Brown Clark and Darlene Simmon's rendition of the spiritual "Calvary" with Richard Smallwood & Vison.[17] There is a world of difference in the feeling and spirit of these two styles. One has tried to come directly to the banquet table, and the other has traveled there through the valley of the shadow of death.

---

[16]Ronald Radano, "On Ownership and Value, *Black Music Research Journal* 30, no. 2 (2010): 363-70.

[17]See "Calvary - Hillsong Worship," YouTube video, 4:22, posted by "Hillsong Worship," June 28, 2017, www.youtube.com/watch?v=qlW_ulQ_-QQ; and "Richard Smallwood & Vision - Calvary," YouTube video, 7:46, posted by "PrazHymn83," November 18, 2008, www.youtube.com/watch?v=gl7kCi2MUsg.

4

STRENGTH TO CLIMB

THE GOSPEL DURING SLAVERY

The slaves developed an Afro-American and Christian

humanism that affirmed joy in the face of every trial.

EUGENE GENOVESE

How did joy emerge in the Black experience of slavery? How can we even make such an audacious claim, when all of the evidence would seem to run counter to its emergence? Consider the words of the great spiritual "Lord Don't Move the Mountain," which asks for "strength to climb":

> Now Lord don't move my mountain
>
> But give me the strength to climb
>
> And Lord, don't take away my stumbling blocks
>
> But lead me all around.[1]

---

[1] Listen to the great Mahalia Jackson's version composed with Doris Akers in 1958: "Lord Don't Move the Mountain - Mahalia Jackson w/ choir," YouTube video, 3:01, posted by "Rowoches," July 17, 2009, www.youtube.com/watch?v=a3AsPjDtmTQ. Consider also Callie Day and Lan Wilson's rendition of *I Know the Lord Will Make a Way*: "Callie Day & Lan Wilson - I Know The Lord Will . . . ," YouTube video, 4:40, posted by "Landen Wilson," August 16, 2014, www.youtube.com/watch?v=6RCQTiCm2ac. See also Harvard scholar

I will argue that much of the joy that developed in Black life and that is expressed in jazz is owed to the Christian message. In the gospel message, Black slaves found a story that resonated with their own experience: Jesus was despised and rejected, he suffered betrayal and desertion, and he was killed by authorities. Yet in his resurrection, he overcame not only worldly powers, but death itself to demonstrate his victory on behalf of the faithful people of God. The "mountains" in African American experience did not often move, but God was there to impart the strength to climb them. The struggle to overcome hindrances is deeply embedded in jazz music. How extensively did the message penetrate jazz? Such a question is important, not least because of the place of spirituals and blues in the background of jazz, and the role of the church in the consciousness of enslaved Africans who became African Americans. But how exactly did the gospel message influence the life and arts of this people?

A MODERN MIRACLE

The adaptation of Africans to the New World was characterized throughout by the Christian message.[2] As we have seen, Christianity was often misused to justify slaveowners' sinful practices. And yet, at various points, slaves embraced the gospel in large numbers. Some have considered this one of the great "miracles" of modern history: slaves recognized a difference between the Christ of the Bible and the hypocritical practice of the preachers, who were often anything but Christlike. As Genovese notes, slaves were painfully aware of the contradiction between a belief in a good God and their owners' cruel and obstinate slaveholding.[3] The team of Sylvia R. Frey and Betty Wood put it in terms of a historiographical

---

Henry Louis Gates Jr.'s *The Black Church: This Is Our Story, This Is Our Song* (New York: Penguin Books, 2021).

[2]The histories of the gospel's influence on enslaved, then free, Africans have been abundant. There is an enormous body of literature on the subject. The interested reader is directed to the appendix on this subject.

[3]Eugene D. Genovese, *Roll, Jordan, Roll: The World the Slaves Made* (New York: Vintage Books, 1976), 191.

paradox: they argue that the conversion of African Americans to Protestant Christianity is perhaps *the* defining moment in their history, and yet this is a nearly forgotten chapter in eighteenth-century Southern intellectual history.[4] But they boldly assert: "[Christianity] created a community of faith and provided a body of values and a religious commitment that became in time the principal solvent of ethnic differences and the primary source of cultural identity."[5] After nearly exhaustive research, the scholar-librarian Dena Epstein concludes, "One can hardly overstate the importance of conversion to Christianity in the acculturation of blacks in the new world."[6]

As to the Christian influence on slave life, there are numerous valuable accounts. Two studies among many are worthy of our attention. First, Albert J. Raboteau's *Slave Religion* looks at every aspect of life in times of slavery, and he is quite mindful of both historical specifics and general trends.[7] Raboteau describes both the emptying of cultural practices from Africa and their possible retentions in the New World.[8] *Slave Religion* includes splendid sections on music, particularly the role of spirituals in slave life.[9] The second study is the more modern account of *The Black Church* by Henry Louis Gates Jr.[10] Gates describes, with elaborate detail, the rise of Black independence both denominationally and in cultural practice. Among his foci, he pays particular attention to the Methodist Episcopal Church, which often set the pace in fostering Black autonomy. He stresses the role of individual leaders, such as Richard Allen during the Awakenings in the move toward independency,[11] and

---

[4]See Sylvia R. Frey and Betty Wood, *Come Shouting to Zion: African American Protestantism in the American South and British Caribbean to 1830* (Chapel Hill: University of North Carolina Press, 1998), 1.

[5]Frey and Wood, *Come Shouting.*

[6]Dena J. Epstein, *Sinful Tunes and Spirituals: Black Folk Music to the Civil War* (Chicago: University of Chicago Press, 2003), 100.

[7]Albert J. Raboteau, *Slave Religion: The "Invisible Institution" in the Antebellum South* (New York: Oxford University Press, 1978).

[8]Raboteau, *Slave Religion*, 53.

[9]Raboteau, *Slave Religion*, 73-74, 246-50, 251-65.

[10]Gates, *Black Church.*

[11]Gates, *Black Church*, 40-52.

he brings us right up to date with challenges such as White violence, Covid, and the megachurch.[12]

Even so, the exact chronology of the Christian influence on the slaves is somewhat elusive. First, it is easy to forget, as we have already mentioned, that the biblical message was present on the African continent long before modern slavery and the conversions of enslaved Africans. Second, traditional African religions were abundant as well, and they were often quite varied. There is still much to learn about them, particularly since the few contemporary chronicles we have lack serious attempts to understand these local religions. Third, the motives of White people leading slaves to faith were mixed at best. There was even a lively debate about whether conversion made slaves more responsible as workers or more prone to rebellion.[13]

THE GOSPEL MAGNETISM

What drew slaves to the gospel? Why would an enslaved people be drawn to the faith of their enslavers? Certain historical developments should be noted. We know that by the seventeenth century some conversions were taking place because of the impact of the beliefs and practices of families who owned slaves. The first organized approach to convert the enslaved Africans to the Christian faith was within the Anglican Church. In 1701, this body created the Society for the Propagation of the Gospel in Foreign Parts (SPG). The first missionary of the SPG, the Rev. Samuel Thomas, was commissioned July 3, 1702, and according to his correspondence a handful of Black people were taught to read and became familiar with the Christian faith. Significantly, the most serious opposition to his efforts, and those of his successors, came from the slave owners and especially the foremen, and this hostility continued well into the eighteenth century. All kinds of

---

[12]Gates, *Black Church*, 186-96.

[13]One particularly disturbing source, although not unusual for its time, is Charles Colcock Jones, *The Religious Instruction of the Negroes in the United States* (Savannah, GA: Thomas Purse, 1842), 124-38, 145-53, in which the author asserts the near impossibility of bringing the gospel to slaves and the "problem" of indigence and moral laxness of Black people in slavery.

reasons were given, including the notion that if slaves became believers they would have to be treated as human beings.

Then came the Great Awakening, spearheaded by dissenters from Anglicanism, such as Presbyterians, Baptists, and Methodists. This remarkable revival of the 1730s and 1740s featured, among other interests, a missionary concern for Black people and Native Americans, as seen in Jonathan Edwards's ministry among Indigenous people. Among the notable individuals with a burden to see slaves converted was Samuel Davies, a Presbyterian from Hanover, Virginia. As he put it, he saw Ethiopia stretch forth her hands unto God. He requested Bibles and hymnals edited by Isaac Watts, which were a great success among the slaves. Again, there was considerable enthusiasm among Black people, but often strong opposition from the planters. The planters were a class of workers, often good businessmen, who often moved onto the plantation property. Though themselves owning slaves, they sometimes sympathized with the enslaved Africans.

Another ray of light is found in the work of American poet Henry Wadsworth Longfellow (1807–1882), who became famous for his epic *The Song of Hiawatha* and who was a fierce opponent of slavery. Unlike Ralph Waldo Emerson and others, Longfellow did not believe that American literature needed to start from scratch, in keeping with the status of the new nation.[14] He published *Poems on Slavery* in 1842, which was remarkably prescient, and he "walked the walk," as he used a good part of the proceeds from *Hiawatha* for the secret liberation of several slaves.[15]

Sadly, this was an exception. In spite of the attempts of abolitionists, and in the face of a few contrarian leaders, race relations did not necessarily ameliorate because of the gospel. Importantly, a few Black independent churches were established in the eighteenth century. The first truly indigenous African American church was led by George Leile in 1773 in Savannah, Georgia.[16] The first Black denomination was founded by Richard

---

[14]See Nicholas Basbanes, *Cross of Snow: A Life of Henry Wadsworth Longfellow* (New York: Knopf, 2020) 34, 57.

[15]Basbanes, *Cross of Snow*, 269.

[16]First African Baptist Church was officially organized in 1788. See the history page on their website, www.firstafricanbc.com/history.php.

Allen and his colleagues, who established the African Methodist Episcopal Church in 1794 in Philadelphia, mostly out of frustration for the way Black people were treated in the Methodist Episcopal Church. Though this denomination grew considerably and gave Black people a real sense of dignity, trouble was never very far away. One day Allen was stopped by a slave-catcher who claimed the African preacher was a runaway. This deceptive practice was fairly common. The man picked the wrong victim, and Allen pulled out his identification papers and then had him arrested and sent to jail. Soon after, Allen intervened and had the man set free. The sad part of the story is not only that it happened at all, but that soon after the whole incident was dismissed and forgotten as an unfortunate mistake.[17]

The next century saw several significant developments for the spread of the gospel among Black people. Among the most remarkable was the camp meeting. Flourishing in prewar years but continuing in various forms up to the twentieth century, these gatherings were often large and literally held in camps outside of the city. Although racial differences were woven into the fabric and not completely overcome, these meetings displayed something approaching racial equality, at least for those times. Black leaders and preachers intermingled with Whites. Among other things, songs and singing traditions were shared. One scholar calls the sociology of these meetings "democratic noise."[18] Whatever the background, class, or economic status of those gathered, when the time for worship came, there was a palpable equality (Gal 3:28). There was significant opposition to these ecstatic expressions, but the witness is still unmistakable.

GROWING DISAPPROVAL

Anti-slavery and abolition movements developed before and after the Civil War. Some advocated a return to Africa, giving birth to various Black

---

[17]See Carole V. R. George, *Segregated Sabbaths: Richard Allen and the Rise of Independent Black Churches 1760–1840* (New York: Oxford University Press, 1973), 3-4.

[18]Keith Dwayne Lyon, "God's Brush Arbor: Camp Meeting Culture During the Second Great Awakening, 1800–1860" (PhD diss., University of Tennessee, 2016), chap. 5.

nationalist movements. Liberia was created at this time. Marcus Garvey
(1887–1940), a Jamaican Roman Catholic, tried to nurture Black unity and
self-determination in journalism and in business. He founded the Universal Negro Improvement Association and preached "pan-Africanism,"
the view that all who belong to the African diaspora share a common
identity and a common vision for the future.

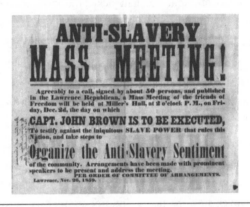

Figure 4.1. Poster for an abolitionist meeting in Lawrence, Kansas, organized
for December 2, 1859, the day of the execution of John Brown, an abolitionist
who was killed for leading a raid at Harpers Ferry

In the late nineteenth and early twentieth centuries, diversification occurred in the church. Various Holiness movements and Pentecostal de-
nominations arose. Alongside these, the great migration north brought
thousands of freed Black people to urban areas such as Chicago and New
York, hoping to find work and societies with fewer prejudices. Though
often disappointed in the realities they encountered, Black people established several notable institutions—such as the Abyssinian Baptist Church
in Harlem, which quickly became a hub of creative and political activity.[19]
Women in particular rose into leadership and guided the churches in religious matters and community action. One thinks of Rosa Horn

---

[19]Abyssinian Baptist Church even had an international impact, as a young Dietrich Bonhoef-
fer was drawn to the preaching of Adam Clayton Powell there and even became a lay leader
during his seminary years in New York.

(1880–1976), who moved from South Carolina to Illinois. Her *Radio Church of God of the Air* programs, which began in 1934, led the way to a savvier use of media by Christians. Nearly all of them featured choirs and used gospel music to great effect. For example, God's House, which is deeply rooted in the Pentecostal tradition, combines exuberant worship with concerns for mental health, community welfare, and even law enforcement. It is intentionally multiracial and multicultural.

But the most significant connection between the gospel and the Black church in North America in recent decades has been the civil rights movement. Advocates such as James M. Lawson, Martin Luther King Jr., and Rosa Parks intentionally connected their remonstration against segregation with biblical principles.[20] For example, in his "Letter from Birmingham Jail," in which he defends the practice of nonviolent but direct action, King cites the prophet Amos: "But let justice roll down like waters, and righteousness like an ever-flowing stream" (Amos 5:3).[21] This and other biblical citations were part and parcel of the oratory of civil rights leaders.

Not everyone was on board. Some objected to the civil rights movement as a White, northern intrusion. On the other side, more radical voices, such as that of Malcolm X, thought the gospel had become so *White* as to make rejection of the church a necessity. In more recent years, Black theologians such as James Cone and womanists such as Marla Frederick have continued to explore the complexity of the relationship between the Christian faith and the Black experience. Cone, a strong advocate of honest faith, has considered the importance of suffering to the Black narrative:

> Suffering naturally gives rise to doubt. How can one believe in God in the face of such horrendous suffering as slavery, segregation, and

---

[20]Many histories of the civil rights movement exist. Among the most accessible are Adam Fairclough, *To Redeem the Soul of America: The Southern Christian Leadership Conference and Martin Luther King Jr.* (Athens: University of Georgia Press, 2002); David Garrow, *Bearing the Cross: Martin Luther King Jr. and the Southern Christian Leadership Conference* (New York: W. Morrow, 1986).

[21]Martin Luther King Jr., *The Gospel of Freedom* (London: Bloomsbury, 2014), 83.

the lynching tree? Under these circumstances, doubt is not a denial but an integral part of faith. It keeps faith from being sure of itself. But doubt does not have the final word. The final word is faith giving rise to hope.[22]

Meanwhile, Frederick is critical of shortcomings that she perceives within White evangelicalism:

> Like the white evangelical church during the years of the civil rights struggle, [current evangelicals] nourish a myth and a morality rendered invisible the structural inequalities that continue to exist for Black Americans and other groups, as well as their own collusion in such systems. They enthusiastically support the idea of racial equality, they also nearly universally believe that all obstacles to Black advancement have disappeared.[23]

So let us return to the question above: What drew Black slaves to the gospel? I have noted several historical developments that point to the complex narrative of the gospel and the Black church. Such experiences must be heard and reckoned with. Yet, in my view, what primarily drew Black slaves to the Christian message was first and foremost the narrative of Jesus Christ, the Son of God made flesh, who died and rose again—a gospel imprinted on their hearts and minds by the Holy Spirit. And it is this narrative that resonated so deeply with slave narratives and the development of Black music.

SLAVE NARRATIVES

A close reading of slave narratives reveals the relationship between the Christian message and its expression in Black music. A word of caution, however, is necessary here. Some of these narratives, while riveting, were written in part to get published, and thus they may reflect a degree of restraint on the part of the authors. Ironically, the reason for that is that the

---

[22]James Cone, *The Cross and the Lynching Tree* (Maryknoll, NY: Orbis Books, 2011), 88.

[23]From a panel discussion sponsored by Harvard Divinity School between Marla F. Frederick and D. Michael Lindsay, "What Do We Really Know About Evangelicals and American Politics?" (March 30, 2021), https://hds.harvard.edu/news/2021/03/30/video-what-do-we-really-know-about-evangelicals-and-american-politics#.

abolitionists, who were largely responsible for publishing most of these narratives, insisted that they appear both factually accurate and that they be consistently negative about slavery, all in order to appeal to the largely White readership.[24]

Thus, the authors had to be careful not to reinforce racial stereotypes while at the same time articulating the horrors of slavery. This has led more contemporary authors to create fresh narratives. A fascinating though neglected study by Shannon E. Hill, "'Free at Last': The Use of Slave Narrative in Ishmael Reed's *Flight to Canada* and Toni Morrison's *Beloved*," shows that the slave narratives can be untangled from some of these constraints because of the more modern outlook of contemporary writers, while yet keeping their voice and understanding them in context.[25] Thus, Hill argues, we have authentic, albeit modern, narratives that consciously seek to "liberate [the slave narrative] from the fetters of the predominant white culture that attempted to frame its creation."[26]

Nevertheless, the original narratives are very moving, and they tend to include common elements.[27] Most significantly, they are all forthrightly Christian. The authors acquired literacy, all of them under circumstances that made such learning dangerous. Literacy gave access to the Bible. Of course, many slave owners did not want their slaves to learn about human dignity and human freedom, which Scripture clearly affirms. Often, opposition to knowledge of the Bible or even conversion was a slippery slope argument that fed on the fear that beginning with freedom in Christ could then lead to physical freedom.[28]

---

[24]See Reymond Hedin, "Muffled Voices: The American Slave Narrative," *Clio* 10 (Winter 1981): 131.

[25]Shannon E. Hill, "'Free at Last': The Use of Slave Narrative in Ishmael Reed's *Flight to Canada* and Toni Morrison's *Beloved*" (AB thesis, Harvard University, 1991).

[26]Hill, "Free at Last," 53.

[27]Frederick Douglass, *Narrative of the Life of Frederick Douglass, an American Slave* (New York: Simon & Brown, 2013); Sojourner Truth, *Narrative of Sojourner Truth, with "Book of Life" and "A Memorial Chapter"* (New York: Barnes & Noble Classics, 2005); Olaudah Equiano, *The Interesting Narrative and Other Writings* (New York: Penguin Classics, 1995); and Solomon Northup, *Twelve Years a Slave* (Melbourne: Golding Books, 2018).

[28]See the chapter on slavery in Alec Ryrie, *Protestants: The Faith That Made the Modern World* (New York: Penguin Books, 2017), 191.

Several of these slave narratives provide insights into the origins and development of jazz. Olaudah Equiano, known as Gustavus Vassa (1745–1797), was an African who was enslaved as a child. He was baptized into the Anglican Church in 1759. Later, he was freed from slavery, and he made his way to England in about 1768. He became a tireless abolitionist and a frontrunner in the Sons of Africa organization. He came to the attention of William Wilberforce and Thomas Clarkson, leaders in the parliamentary movement that later abolished slavery in the British Empire in 1833. Equiano is best remembered today for his *Interesting Narrative* (1789). While references to music in Olaudah Equiano's writings are sparse, he provided the following memorable description:

> We are almost a nation of dancers, musicians, and poets. Thus, every great event, such as a triumphant return from battle, or other cause of public rejoicing, is celebrated in public dances, which are accompanied with songs and music suited to the occasion. The assembly is separated into four divisions, which dance either apart or in succession, and each with a character peculiar to itself. The first division contains the married men, who, in their dances frequently exhibit feats of arms, and the representation of a battle. To these succeed the married women, who dance in the second division. The young men occupy the third; and the maidens the fourth. Each represents some interesting scene of real life, such as a great achievement, domestic employment, a pathetic story, or some rural sport; and, as the subject is generally founded on some recent event, it is therefore ever new. This gives our dances a spirit and variety which I have scarcely seen elsewhere. We have many musical instruments, particularly drums of different kinds, a piece of music which resembles a guitar, and another much like a stickado. These last are chiefly used by betrothed virgins, who play on them on all grand festivals.[29]

---

[29]Equiano, *Interesting Narrative*, 34. A stickado is an instrument similar to a xylophone.

Such a text tells us much about the social configuration of the slaves and their music.

Sojourner Truth (c. 1797–1883) is the name that was taken by a Dutch-speaking slave, Isabella.[30] Often sold, beaten, and abused, she finally found emancipation in 1827. She became greatly involved with the Pentecostal branch of the Methodist Church and later the Seventh-Day Adventists, becoming a noted preacher, evangelist, abolitionist, and defender of women's rights. Dictated to an editor, *The Narrative of Sojourner Truth, A Northern Slave* was first published in 1850. A singer and composer, she often interspersed her lectures with hymns. At one camp meeting, she sang from the top of a hill a song about the resurrection of Christ, which began this way:

It was early in the morning—it was early in the morning,

Just at the break of day—

When he rose—when he rose—when he rose,

And went to heaven on a cloud.

The editor notes that she sang in a fervent manner with a powerful voice and that those who heard could not separate the tune and style from herself, "with the utmost strength of her most powerful voice."[31] Her favorite themes were freedom and glory:

O righteous Father,

Do look down on me,

And help me on to Canada,

Where colored folks are free.[32]

Her audiences noted how zealously she believed in the reality of heaven. This utter realism about the afterlife is characteristic of African American

---

[30]Truth, *Narrative*.

[31]Truth, *Narrative*, 85-86.

[32]Truth, *Narrative*, 123.

piety, and it finds its way into the music. Many years later, Duke Ellington would perform his own eschatological masterpiece, "Heaven."[33]

The descriptions of human suffering found in the accounts of Frederick Douglass (1817–1895) are harrowing and raw.[34] He notes that with the ability to read came a reliable access to history. Douglass even claimed to envy his fellow slaves for their "stupidity" since his understanding of history and the evils of slavery would "torment and sting my soul."[35] Yet interspersed with such comments is the hopefulness afforded by the gospel.

His references to music are significant, though varied. Importantly, they help us understand the aesthetics of the music—and ultimately why jazz became what it is. Douglass comments that slaves were expected to sing at all times. But though the songs could be wild, they were not necessarily merry: "On the contrary, they were mostly of a plaintive cast, and told a tale of grief and sorrow. In the most boisterous outbursts of rapturous sentiment, there was ever a tinge of deep melancholy."[36] This characteristic of the music became deeply embedded in the music that shaped jazz.

One of the most heartwrenching narratives is Solomon Northup's *Twelve Years a Slave* (1853).[37] Adapted to film in 2013, it is the account of first being a free man, then being kidnapped and forced back into slavery, and finally freed again. Northup writes as a Christian, and at times he sounds rather generous to his oppressors, while still conveying the horrors of slavery. He played the violin, and the accounts of music-making are mostly about being forced to entertain the slavers, who constantly used the whip. In a poignant passage, Northup explains that his people understood freedom and yearned for it, contradicting their oppressors who thought them incapable of such notions. He memorably describes one

---

[33]Listen to the hauntingly beautiful version from his Sacred Concerts: "Duke Ellington's Second Sacred Concert: Heaven (feat Alice Babs & Johnny Hodges)," YouTube video, 5:21, posted by "Esatchmo," July 9, 2014, www.youtube.com/watch?v=rZaW0ubJl0M.

[34]Douglass, *Narrative*.

[35]Douglass, *Narrative*, 160.

[36]Douglass, *Narrative*, 166-67.

[37]Northup, *Twelve Years*.

poor woman who was constantly tortured and saw no difference between heaven and exemption from the whip. She sang this "melancholy bard":

I ask no paradise on high,

With cares on earth oppressed,

The only heaven for which I sigh,

Is rest, eternal rest.[38]

Heaven, in Black theology, once again, is a very real place, a place of consolation and rest.

These and many more testimonies together witness to a number of elements that make up the aesthetics of African American music—elements that would later be found present in jazz music. But above all, they testify to the great Christian narrative that supports and underlies all these narratives: the movement from deep misery to inextinguishable joy.

---

[38]Northup, *Twelve Years*, 98.

PART II

BACKGROUND GENRES

5

RESILIENCE

THE MUSIC OF STRENGTH

It is difficult to express the entire character of these negro ballads

by mere musical notes and signs. The odd turns made in the throat;

the curious rhythmic effect produced by single voices chiming in

at different irregular intervals, seem almost as impossible to place

on score, as the singing of birds or the tones of an Aeolian harp.

LUCY MCKIM GARRISON

As we will see in the next few chapters, Black music took particular forms during and just after slavery, including spirituals, gospel, and the blues. Here we want to mention a few characteristics of the music found in all its forms.[1] Whatever else it was, it was a music of resilience.

Music-making characterized every aspect of the life of slaves. While the emergence of music in every aspect of life is common to many peoples, it was particularly a feature of the life of Black people, perhaps because there were so few other outlets.

Generally speaking, this is less the case in many modern societies. Try to imagine someone behind a desk in an urban office building bursting

---

[1] A good place to look for resources is the Smithsonian Institution: "Roots of African American Music," accessed January 5, 2022, music.si.edu/spotlight/african-american-music/roots-of-african-american-music.

into song or leading everyone in the room to sing. Instead, music is often either privatized (using earpieces) or made formal (the concert or the opera). For slaves and later Black generations, music was created in and for all situations. Making music in all circumstances might be the more extraordinary in that the slaves came from many different backgrounds and met fellow captives only on North American soil.[2]

PROTEST

Because conditions were so dreadfully oppressive, it should surprise no one that one of the general features of much Black music was *protest*. Though cruelly subjugated, there was always something left of the freeborn soul, even during the worst humiliations. Occasionally, resistance and protest took the form of physical, violent rebellion, but these were usually not successful. Slave revolts were fairly regular in North America and the Caribbean Islands. Most were suppressed, though a few may be deemed "victorious."[3] In addition to Tacky's Revolt in Jamaica (1761), three of the most well-known revolts were led by Gabriel Prosser in Virginia (1800), Denmark Vesey in South Carolina (1822), and Nat Turner in Virginia (1831). There were also mutinies such as the *Neptune* (1797) and *La Amistad* (1839).

Music was involved in both the violent insurrections and the quieter inward resistance. Sometimes loud music was played to cover up the breaking of the shackles before an uprising. The more private ones were almost invariably melancholy, reciting the story of the slaves' captivity and their separation from their loved ones. Jazz music often carries with it an element of remonstration. Not only in the intentionally revolutionary sounds of bebop, but even in the earliest styles, jazz music was partly characterized by the desire to offer an alternative to a culture of White preeminence.

---

[2]"African American Song," Library of Congress, accessed January 5, 2022, www.loc.gov/item /ihas.200197451/.
[3]See Herbert Aptheker, *American Negro Slave Revolts*, 5th ed. (New York: International Publishers, 1985).

GOOD SUBVERSION

One of the best-known and most captivating cases of defying oppression is the slaves' response to various laws forbidding drumming and then dance. Drums for Africans not only set the rhythm for their dances and ceremonies but were used for communication. The famous "talking drums" could be heard for miles and were used to signal an open market, a visitor, or the advance of an enemy army. When West Africans came to North America, they were able to continue the practice. Soon, however, the slave owners caught on and started to curtail the use of drums. Fearing the use of drums to tip off their colleagues about an insurrection or a riot, a series of "Black codes" were enacted even further limiting the freedom of the slaves. Article 36 of the South Carolina Slave Code (1740) states:

> It is absolutely necessary to the safety of this Province, that all due care be taken to restrain Negroes from using or keeping of drums, which may call together or give sign or notice to one another of their wicked designs and purposes.[4]

This type of law spread across Georgia, and then most of the South. The one exception, at least for a while, was Louisiana, whose Roman Catholic culture was more permissive than the Protestant evangelical culture of other states.

New Orleans differed greatly from the rest of the young United States in its Old World cultural relationships. The Creole culture was Catholic and French-speaking rather than Protestant and English-speaking. A more liberal outlook on life prevailed, with an appreciation of good food, wine, music, and dancing. Festivals were frequent, and Governor William Claiborne, the first American-appointed governor of the territory of Louisiana, reportedly commented that New Orleanians were ungovernable because of their preoccupation with dancing.[5]

---

[4]See Annie Campbell, "Excerpts from South Carolina Slave Code of 1740 No. 670 (1740)," U.S. History Scene, accessed January 5, 2022, ushistoryscene.com/article/excerpts -south-carolina-slave-code-1740-no-670-1740/.
[5]Joseph F. Stoltz III, "'The Preservation of Good Order': William C. C. Claiborne and the Louisiana Provisional Government, 1803–1805," in *Journal of the Louisiana Historical Association* 54, no. 4 (Fall 2013): 424-25.

But slaves soon realized that they did not need physical drums in order to generate rhythm. Spoons, washboards, furniture, and the human body became their instruments. A technique known as "patting juba" or "hambone" was developed whereby a human being could be made to sound like an entire rhythm section.[6] This is no doubt at the origins of the tap dance and many other forms of foot stomping, as well as different forms of drumless music that made its way into the mainstream, such as ragtime, minstrel songs, blues, and others.[7]

Not only were forms of communication and dance rhythms preserved or reinvigorated through such transfers, but many of them found their way into the church. For example, despite various prohibitions, one dance that was preserved and renovated, not only in Louisiana, but elsewhere, is the "ring shout." As the name implies, this is a style in which participants form a circle, and then clap, stamp their feet, and occasionally burst out in an ecstatic utterance. There is a well-attested story that on at least one occasion the town fathers of New Orleans got nervous about dancing on Congo Square. In response, they issued a decree forbidding the dance in Black gatherings. But not to be outdone, the Black dancers asked them to define the dance, so they would know what not to do. After several days in committee, they came out with the following definition: dance is when you cross your legs. They agreed not to do that and proceeded to create all kinds of "non-dance" movements, including the ring shout.[8]

---

[6]You can see and hear this practice. Danny "Slapjazz" Barber is among the best: "Danny 'Slapjazz' Barber - #BodyMusic @ #IBMF 11," YouTube video, 1:26, posted by "Body Music Festival," September 2, 2013, www.youtube.com/watch?v=cTnWWiex7DU.

[7]See, for example, "JUBA DANCE: The dance of African slaves in American plantations," YouTube video, 2:07, posted by "FREE STEP ITALIA OFFICIAL," July 18, 2017, www.youtube .com/watch?v=hpNdQDWgy7I.

[8]See William Barlow, *Looking Up at Down: The Emergence of Blues Culture* (Philadelphia: Temple University Press, 1989), 48-50. One Louisiana man testified that "dancin' ain't sinful iffen de foots ain't crossed"; see Burton W. Peretti, *The Creation of Jazz: Music, Race, and Culture in Urban America* (Urbana: University of Illinois Press, 1992), 16. There is an extensive literature on the ring shout. One can see contemporary forms of it from the Gullah people, particularly in Mcintosh County and other Georgia islands: "Plantation Dance Ring Shout," YouTube video, 3:10, posted by "mhenrystl," May 1, 2016, www.youtube.com /watch?v=NQgrIcCtys0.

The call-and-response patterns common to West Africa and the British Isles was another regular feature of Black music. As religious historian Albert Raboteau comments, in tent meetings, Black worshipers bridged African traditions with appeals to the Christian God, resulting in the "holy dance."[9] As he adds, certain restrictions still applied. For example, crossing one's feet violated decorum.[10]

HUMOR AS PROTEST

Protest is serious, but it must not always mean joylessness. As suggested above, protest is not unconnected with a certain kind of Black joy. There is something in the spirit of the best jazz music, which combines the two: joy and protest. And this combination originated during slavery. But a good deal of caution is called for, particularly to avoid the racist idea mentioned earlier that Black people are inevitably "happy." As noted previously, the display of merriment through song and dance was frequent. Yet mostly, it was a façade, giving the impression of cheerfulness, when in fact there was nothing to be cheerful about. Underneath the façade there was often an awareness of incredible injustice and the need to subvert it. Neil Leonard draws attention to the "zaniness" of the prophetic figure who was the jazz musician.[11]

Talented musicians earned a degree of respect both before and after the Civil War. A good instrumentalist was known as a "musicianer" and could be counted on for parties and even for church services. One standard form of entertainment was the *frolic*, which could be a fish fry, a picnic, or any kind of house party.[12] Many of the musicians were self-taught, though they could pass on their skills to ensuing generations. The banjo was one

---

[9]Albert J. Raboteau, *Slave Religion: The "Invisible Institution" in the Antebellum South* (New York: Oxford University Press, 1978), 73. He adds that ring shouts could be called "running sperichils," a term that meant to connect the dance with spirituals. See this performance of "Tree of Life": "Weeksville Heritage Center," YouTube video, 6:14, posted by "Mireille Long," July 8, 2012, www.youtube.com/watch?v=DOJj_MNIBUg.
[10]Raboteau, *Slave Religion*, 539-40n69.
[11]Neil Leonard, *Jazz, Myth and Religion* (New York: Oxford University Press, 1987), 39.
[12]See Paul A. Cimbala, "Black Musicians from Slavery to Freedom: An Exploration of an African-American Folk Elite and Cultural Continuity in the Nineteenth Century Rural South," *Journal of Negro History* 80, no. 1 (1993): 15-28.

of the prominent instruments, and audiences participated through clapping, foot stomping, and general sharing.

By the time of the advent of jazz music, the posture of the "happy performer" was near commonplace. Yet it had already become the subject of debate. Audiences can easily misinterpret a smiling entertainer or an exuberant performer as a truly joyful person. Yes, there can be great joyfulness in jazz, but the best jazz is not especially happy.[13] The one is merriment or glee, the other is a deep sense of jubilation and contentment.

In the world of jazz, musicians often had to subvert the expectations of White audiences. Today, comedians owe much of their style to the characters spread across African American history. In the nineteenth century, one of the most popular figures was the *trickster*. Possibly harking back to African culture, the trickster grew to mythic proportions on American soil. He was at once a kind of survivor and even a judge. He was a comic who outwitted his opponents. He was often an animal character, and perhaps the best-known trickster was Brer Rabbit, who outsmarted Brer Fox by telling him there was a hunk of cheese at the bottom of a well. The fox goes down, the rabbit goes up.

Often the tales of tricksters carried a moral lesson. In the 1880s, Charles Waddell Chesnutt created an anthology in which a raconteur, a survivor from slave times, tells of the Conjure Woman, a trickster who is able to transform people into different objects of disguise. In one tale, a slave survives because the Conjure Woman turns him into a tree, planted successively in different locations. Unfortunately, a local sawmill decides to cut him down.[14] This kind of tale was told to White people and meant both to underscore the cruelty of slavery and the need for current democratic equality.

Another well-known trickster was the Black figure Stagolee.[15] Apparently, on Christmas night in 1895, there was a gathering at the Bill Curtis

---

[13]A similar point using different terms was made by Angelina Grimké, a women's rights activist, who says slaves may exhibit mirth but never happiness. See Angelina Grimké Weld, *Speech at Pennsylvania Hall* (1837), www.pbs.org/wgbh/aia/part4/4h2939t.html.

[14]Charles Waddell Chestnut, "The Conjure Woman," in *Stories, Novels and Essays* (Washington, DC: Library of America, 2002) 62-77.

[15]Cecil Brown, *Stagolee Shot Billy* (Cambridge, MA: Harvard University Press, 2004).

Saloon in St. Louis. Lee Shelton, known as "Stack Lee," a local pimp, walked in and started a discussion with Bill Lyons, a young Black levee worker, who was known as a bully. Things degenerated and they broke into a fight over politics, and Lee damaged Billy's derby hat. Billy tried but failed to grab Lee's Stetson. Lee then was baited into shooting him. Lee survived one court trial but then got into trouble again and went to prison, where he died. By then he had become a hero, a trickster. He was hailed by writers including Carl Sandburg, Gwendolyn Brooks, Richard Wright, and James Baldwin and by musicians such as Ma Rainey, Sidney Bechet, Bo Diddley, Bob Dylan, and the Clash. Even Elvis Presley and Jerry Lee Lewis have their versions of the song dedicated to him. For some, Stagolee is a favorite Black folk hero whose story amounts to nothing short of a defining social drama.[16]

While justified violence was the storyline for some African Americans, often protest took more subtle and layered forms, using double entendre. Yet from this form of protest, and from the oppressive world Black people often lived in, the wonderful music of jazz emerged. As Nathan B. Young puts it, "Out of the 'Chestnut Valley' came the most beautiful music. Out of the green scum and muck grow the fairest lilies and valuable hardwood trees; out of old Chestnut Valley sprang the stock of popular American music, nurtured and flavored by Negro musicians. . . . American ragtime, out of which the blues and swing music evolved, should have a St. Louis label on it."[17]

Decades later, Black musicians continued a form of protest by out-smarting their audiences as well as their employers. Duke Ellington, ar-guably the most celebrated jazz composer of all time, found himself playing before White audiences who expected him to play "jungle music," such as the song "Echoes of the Jungle."[18] He developed the sound inten-sively during his years at the Cotton Club in Harlem (1927–1932). To our

---

[16]See Cecil Brown, *Stagolee Shot Billy* (Cambridge, MA: Harvard University Press, 2004).

[17]Chestnut Valley was a tough section of the city of St. Louis. Nathan B. Young, "Some Basic Cultural Developments," in *Ain't but a Place*, ed. Gerald Early (St. Louis: St. Louis Historical Society, 1999), 339. The best study to date of the trickster myth is no doubt John W. Roberts, *From Trickster to Badman: The Black Folk Hero in Slavery and Freedom* (Philadelphia: University of Pennsylvania Press, 1989).

[18]"Duke Ellington Cotton Club Orch. - Echoes Of The Jungle, 1931," YouTube video, 3:28, posted by "240252," February 19, 2008, www.youtube.com/watch?v=vYNwiAXuh_U.

ears, there may not be much "jungle" here, but the solos on trumpet, saxo-phone, and violin were a sort of subversive way of fooling the audience. Then, as if to subvert the subversion, Duke continued to develop a love for Africa and to compose songs in an African vein, including *Little African Flower* and *The Mooch*.[19]

Other examples of humor abound. One may think of the amazing Cab Calloway's antics. In his bestselling hit "Minnie the Moocher," he breaks into "scat" singing, using nonsense words in a call-and-response pattern. Minnie was apparently a real person named Minnie Gayton, a homeless woman from Indianapolis who had died, frozen to death in a blizzard. This hardly sounds humorous, but it was a comical song because of Cal-loway's riff on Minnie's fantasy world:

She had a dream about the king of Sweden;

he gave her things, that she was needin'.

He gave her a home built of gold and steel,

a diamond car, with the puh-latinum wheels.

Hi-de-hi-de-hi-de-hi-de-hi-de-hi-de-hi

Ho-de-ho-de-ho-de-ho-de-ho-de-oh

Skeedle-a-booka-diki biki skeedly beeka gookity woop!

A-booriki-booriki-booriki Hoy!

As can be imagined, the audience would begin to participate and then get lost in the attempt.[20] At one level, this is just great amusement, but it was also a way of subverting the audience.

Thus, humor is an important part of the jazz aesthetic. But, we insist, not just any humor. A number of trumpet players have mastered the

---

[19]Other memorable songs in this genre include "Creole Love Call," "The Blues I Love to Sing," and "Black and Tan Fantasy." For a helpful analysis of Duke's relation to the so-called jungle sound, see John Franceschina, *Duke Ellington's Music for the Theater* (Jefferson, NC: McFarland, 2001), 11-27.

[20]Calloway recorded the piece numerous times, including in the film *Blues Brothers*.

"wah-wah" sound using a plunger, producing humorous sounds. The *Livery Stable Blues* features whinnying and neighing sounds on the clarinet, trumpet, and trombone. James P. Johnson, the marvelous Harlem pianist, played a piece called "You've Gotta Be Modernistic," in which he plays a series of whole-tone chords to ragtime. The whole-tone scale was considered a motif for modern times.[21] Horace Silver's last recorded album, *Jazz Has a Sense of Humor*, includes songs such as "The Mama Suite" and "Philley Millie," in which the pianist mixes excellent musicianship with just outright silliness.[22]

Another kind of humor for those "in the know" is the use of quotes. Musicians love to throw citations from various sources into their improvisations. Dizzy Gillespie liked to insert a brief clip from "Habanera" from Bizet's Carmen into numerous solos. Hassan Shakur (J. J. Wiggins) has a bass routine where he throws in familiar lines such as "Eleanor Rigby," the theme from *The Pink Panther*, and the "Axel F" theme from *Beverly Hills Cop*. Of course, they all fit into the harmony and rhythm of the piece.[23] It is best to think of the presence of humor in jazz as an extension of its joyfulness, which can be a part of protest. But let's not rob the music of its amusement, either. It's okay to laugh!

FRESH AND REAL

Another important feature of jazz was that it was fresh. One writer calls jazz "risky, scary, dangerous."[24] He is not claiming jazz leads to insurrection, but that it is based on improvisation, which leaves the performer without props like sheet music. How did it come to be so creative? There are many reasons, but one factor was that African slaves were taken from

---

[21]"You've Got to Be Modernistic," YouTube video, 3:09, posted by "James P. Johnson's Harmony Eight - Topic," November 20, 2015, www.youtube.com/watch?v=VKJFzdSkZgg.

[22]"Philley Millie," YouTube video, 4:45, posted by "Horace Silver - Topic," July 30, 2018, www.youtube.com/watch?v=U62FtRwyMS4.

[23]See, for example, "Monty Alexander Trio Plus," YouTube video, 7:12, posted by "Marlon Domingus," September 7, 2013, www.youtube.com/watch?v=DCkSq0OpEXs.

[24]Moira E. McLaughlin, "All About Jazz, Uniquely American Music," KidsPost, *Washington Post*, May 24, 2012, www.washingtonpost.com/lifestyle/style/all-about-jazz-a-unique -form-of-american-music/2012/05/24/gJQA4bswnU_story.html.

numerous tribal backgrounds, and when they were coerced into dancing and making music, they had to blend their traditions. The use of drums, for example, varied greatly from tribe to tribe. But in order to perform as one, a certain syncretism was necessary. This unity was preserved in the New World, which is why African American music is not simply composed of retentions from Africa.[25] The freshness is not only because of a combination of styles, but because of the unique circumstances that enslaved Africans encountered in the New World.

If jazz aesthetics is the product of deep misery followed by inextinguishable joy, then a principal generator for this aesthetic was the Christian message. As we have seen, slave narratives provide rich insights into the way spiritual music was part of the life of the slave. The gospel penetrated Black life through evangelism, Bible literacy, camp meetings, and civil rights initiatives. Jazz, then, is an extension and an expression of the Black community that was so deeply shaped by the Christian message. The message that was so horribly misused and abused by some to justify the enslavement of others also encouraged originality by calling people to "sing a new song" (Ps 96:1) and to see themselves as a "new creation" in Christ (2 Cor 5:17).

---

[25]See Philip D. Morgan, *Slave Counterpoint: Black Culture in the Eighteenth Century Chesapeake and Lowcountry* (Chapel Hill: University of North Carolina Press, 1998), 418-20, 581-94.

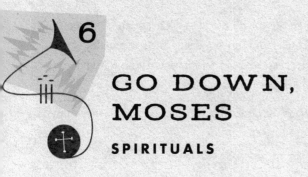

6

GO DOWN, MOSES

SPIRITUALS

Faith in the righteousness of God was not easy

for black people, since God's liberating work

in the world was not always completely evident.

JAMES CONE

The movement from misery to joy in Black music was an echo of many Bible stories, centering on worship. Though often the worship of God was considered illegal or subversive, many slaves who were believers found ways to worship God clandestinely. At the edge of the plantation, one could find log cabins that became "hush houses." Slaves would gather two-by-two, carrying buckets of water and large sheets, which would be nailed to the walls and doused with water for makeshift soundproofing. Then the preacher would preach, moving from speech to cantillation and interacting with the gathered congregation. According to various accounts, this became the chief birthplace of the Negro spiritual. The following testimony from a hush house recounts a preacher's exposition on Ezekiel's account of the dry bones:

> He'd splain de word and read what Ezekiel done say—Dry bones
> gwine ter lib again. And, honey, de Lord would come a-shining

> thoo dem pages and revive dis ole n[——]'s heart, and I'd jump up
> dar and den and holler and shout and sing and pat, and dey would
> all cotch de words . . . and dey's all take it up and keep at it, and keep
> a-addin to it *and den it would be a spiritual.*[1]

This is an extraordinary account of the birth of one of the most moving
and universally beloved styles of music.

"LET'S SING . . ."

Spirituals were born out of the Black experience and in the Black church,
both invisible and visible. In addition to these clandestine meetings, there
were more open ones. Black people were invited into White churches, but
in a reflection of social realities that deny the unity of the people of God
(Eph 4:4), they had to sit in the back or in the balconies. Yet, even here,
there was surprising and considerable creativity. One well-documented
example is the Black adaptation of European psalm singing. Reformer
John Calvin believed congregations should sing mostly psalms, arguing
that these were divinely authorized prayers. He further argued that they
should be a cappella (without instruments), because instruments be-
longed to the Old Testament economy.[2] One of the results of this approach
was the devising of a way of singing that kept the music moving along,
called "lining out." A precentor, or lead singer, would line out a
verse, then the congregation would sing it back. Strangely and wonderfully, when Black slaves heard this, they loved it. First, the sounds were

---

[1]Jeannette Robinson Murphy, "The Survival of African Music in America," *Popular Science Monthly* 55 (1899): 329, https://archive.org/details/SurvivalOfAfricanMusicInAmerica. Ital-ics mine. See also John W. Work, *American Negro Songs* (Minneola, NY: Dover, 1998); Dena J. Epstein, *Sinful Tunes and Spirituals: Black Folk Music to the Civil War* (Urbana: University of Illinois Press, 2003); Laurie Treat, *The Creation of Negro Spirituals: An Enno-bling Power of Survival* (independently published, 2019); Howard Thurman, *Deep River: An Interpretation of Negro Spirituals* (Whitefish, MT: Kessinger, 2010).

[2]His and other arguments for "exclusive psalmody" included the belief that Christ had ful-filled the Old Testament's practices and that now music should be "from the heart" but without instruments. See Charles Garsides Jr., *The Origins of Calvin's Theology of Music 1536–1543*, Transactions 69/4 (Philadelphia: American Philosophical Society, 1979), 26. See also C. McMahon, ed., *The Puritans on Exclusive Psalmody* (Crossville, TN: Puritan, 2013); Karin Maag, *Worshiping with the Reformers* (Downers Grove, IL: IVP Academic, 2021).

modal (think of Gregorian chant or playing only the black keys on a piano), much like African music. Second, lining out was antiphonal—that is, using a call-and-response pattern—a widespread practice in West African music. Third, the singing was extremely slow. But rather than be frustrated, the slaves began to improvise with vocal glides, grace notes, falsetto, and blue notes. This tradition has continued down to the present in African American song. For example, when Aretha Franklin sings "Amazing Grace," it might take her five minutes to get through the first stanza.[3] This style was often introduced as "Let's sing the old Dr. Watts," referring to Isaac Watts, who composed many of the hymns that were sung. When the Black congregation sang "the old Dr. Watts," it was usually not Watts's hymnody, but the lining out technique.[4] Yet both styles could contribute to forming a more Christlike individual and church.

Arthur Singleton, a Victorian adventurer, comments that he saw both practicality and artistry in the songs produced by slaves under duress: "Time and again, whites watched almost uncomprehendingly as slaves used sound and coordinated bodily movements to turn work into performance."[5] Scholars Shane White and Graham White comment that the desire to turn work into performance can be evidenced throughout African American history. They cite the example of convicts singing to a rhythmic movement. Zora Neale Hurston concurs with her "dynamic suggestion" mentioned earlier, in which a Black dancer merely suggests movement that the audience may then infer.[6]

---

[3]Numerous recordings exist. The haunting song "Dark Was the Night" was interpreted by Mary Price: "Dark Was the Night," YouTube video, 1:15, posted by "Mary Price - Topic," May 24, 2015, www.youtube.com/watch?v=IolJdSGBI2Y. Another version of the same song is by Blind Willie Johnson: "Blind Willie Johnson - Dark was the night . . . ," YouTube video, 3:21, posted by "jovauri," August 7, 2007, www.youtube.com/watch?v =BNj2BXW852g. See Shane White and Graham White, *The Sounds of Slavery: Discovering African American History Through Songs, Sermons, and Speech* (Boston: Beacon, 2005), 62-63.

[4]See H. R. Rookmaaker, "Spirituals and Gospel," in *New Orleans Jazz, Mahalia Jackson and the Philosophy of Art*, ed. Marleen Hengelaar-Rookmaaker, The Complete Works of H. R. Rookmaaker 2 (Carlisle, UK: Piquant, 2002), 338-58.

[5]Robin D. G. Kelley, *Race Rebels: Culture and Politics and the Black Working Class* (New York: Free Press, 1994), 2.

[6]Quoted in White and White, *Sounds of Slavery*, 73.

On the whole, this way of singing was quite different from the European, White vocal approach. Often observers from Europe were caught off guard by the difference, but many were appreciative. Frederick Law Olmstead was a keen observer, recording that the language of the spiritual was "highly metaphorical ... yet, sometimes beautiful." He noted in one service in New Orleans that the "collective sound" was "wonderful" though "unusual," filled with "indescribable expressions of ecstasy."[7]

LIBERATION AND MORE

The message of the spirituals included themes from the Old Testament, the life of Jesus, liberation, and patience through suffering. According to Black theologian James Cone, the theological content and significance of the spiritual were centered on liberation.[8] On the whole, slaves rightly refused to believe that God was on the side of the oppressors. One of the constant themes of spirituals, then, was that God was the great liberator who would reverse the patterns of injustice. A favorite spiritual was "Mary Don't You Weep":

Oh Mary don't you weep, don't you moan,

Oh Mary don't you weep, don't you moan,

Pharaoh's army got drownded,

Oh Mary, don't you weep.[9]

It is interesting to note that in this particular case, various biblical stories were merged in the song, including the story of Lazarus's resurrection and the defeat of the Egyptian army in the Red Sea.

---

[7]White and White, *Sounds of Slavery*, 100.

[8]James H. Cone, *The Spirituals and the Blues* (Maryknoll, NY: Orbis Books, 1972), 3.

[9]Here is the classic version by the Swan Silvertones: "The Swan Silvertones - Oh Mary Don't You Weep," YouTube video, 2:43, posted by "Walter Robinson," August 23, 2013, www.youtube.com/watch?v=d4hdWcxa0lQ. Also listen to Aretha Franklin singing a gospel version of the song in one of the greatest concerts of all time: "Aretha Franklin - Mary, Don't You Weep (Official Audio)," YouTube video, 7:26, posted by "Aretha Franklin," February 10, 2019, www.youtube.com/watch?v=xiChwl_zHiU. Recently, the full service, including all the words of the sermon, etc., has been rediscovered: [Atlantic Catalog Group 1999].

Many other spirituals also recall the theme of liberation. Among the best known are "My Lord Delivered Daniel," "Go Down Moses," and "Freedom." As Cone puts it, "[Black people] rejected white distortions of the gospel, which emphasized the obedience of slaves to their masters. They contended that God willed their freedom and not their slavery."[10] African American theologian Anthony Pinn agrees with much of Cone's assessment, but he argues that there is more *theodicy* in the spirituals than Cone asserts. That is, while there is much about God's trustworthiness in the spirituals, there is also some tension there, a wrestling with the problem of God's goodness in the midst of Black suffering.[11]

Go down Moses

Way down in Egypt land

Tell ol' Pharaoh to

Let my people go!

When Israel was in Egypt land

Let my people go!

Oppressed so hard they could not stand

Let my people go!

So God said: go down, Moses

Way down in Egypt land

Tell ol' Pharaoh to

Let my people go!

So Moses went to Egypt land

Let my people go!

---

[10]Cone, *Spirituals and the Blues*, 33.

[11]Anthony B. Pinn, *Why, Lord? Suffering and Evil in Black Theology* (New York: Continuum, 1995), 33-38. Pinn further argues that slaves were often suspicious of White Christianity and thus sought solace in their own interpretation of Scripture.

He made ol' Pharaoh understand

Let my people go!

Yes the lord said: go down, Moses

Way down in Egypt land

Tell ol' Pharaoh to

Let my people go!

In this way, spirituals applied the biblical narratives to the experience of Black slaves, so the denunciation of Pharoah, the historical oppressor of the Israelites, also entailed the rejection of *all* pharaohs. There are many recordings of this classic spiritual, but, in my view, none is more moving and haunting than Big Mama Thornton's.[12]

My own belief is that the spirituals taken as a whole are not so singularly focused on liberation as Cone contends. Freedom is certainly an important theme. But it perhaps accords too much with Cone's particular brand of liberation theology, which has its virtues, to be sure, but also operates on a specific definition of freedom that many Christians might find insufficiently spiritual or overly materialistic.[13] In my view, the spirituals contain a wider range of theological reflections, all of which, to be sure, reflect the unique Black experience and awareness. There is not only hope for liberation, but there is also comfort—not an escapist comfort, but a biblically based refuge in God's provision through Jesus Christ.

The theme of suffering, which would become an indelible feature of jazz, is especially found in the soul of the spirituals. They often express the haunting question we all have painfully asked like the psalmist: "How long, O Lord?"

O Lord, how long shall the wicked,
   how long shall the wicked exult?

12"Big mama Thornton 'Go Down Moses,'" YouTube video, 4:35, posted by "anthony berrot," February 12, 2010, www.youtube.com/watch?v=CTZ4VyhLZOY.
13See James H. Cone, *A Black Theology of Liberation*, 40th anniversary ed. (Maryknoll, NY: Orbis Books, 2010).

They pour out their arrogant words;
>   all the evildoers boast.
They crush your people, O Lord,
>   and afflict your heritage.
They kill the widow and the sojourner,
>   and murder the fatherless;
and they say, "The Lord does not see;
>   the God of Jacob does not perceive." (Ps 94:3-7)[14]

"Lord, Don't Leave Me," a poignant spiritual, cries out like the psalmist, "Don't leave me, Lord, don't leave me behind." It is then no surprise that the suffering of Jesus, who also cried out to God the Father (Mt 26:39; 27:46) is frequently highlighted in the spirituals, as in "Were You There" and "Mumbalin' Word," also known as "Crucifixion." The spirituals might point to individual suffering and loneliness (for example, "Nobody Knows the Trouble I've Seen," "Motherless Child," or "My Lord, I've Had Many Crosses"), or they may express a desire to flee away to safety, as in "Steal Away" and "We Have a Just God."[15]

But, like the psalms, they also offered responses to such questions and cries. Consider, for example, the response from the psalmist from the same psalm quoted above:

Understand, O dullest of the people!
>   Fools, when will you be wise?
He who planted the ear, does he not hear?
He who formed the eye, does he not see?

---

[14]See also Ps 4:2; 6:3; 13:1; 35:17; 62:3; 79:5; 89:46.

[15]See, for example, "Were You There": "Three Mo' Tenors - Were You There - 7/17/2001 (Official)," YouTube video, 4:42, posted by "Jazz on MV," September 23, 2014, www.youtube .com/watch?v=uhGYD1svTM4; "Crucifixion" by Darryl Taylor: "He Never Said a Mumblin' Word (Crucifixion)," YouTube video, 6:07, posted by "Darryl Taylor - Topic," February 8, 2015, www.youtube.com/watch?v=_b-LxV4MuiI; Louis Armstrong's version of "Nobody Knows": "Louis Armstrong - Nobody Knows the Trouble I've Seen (1962)," YouTube video, 2:32, posted by "wenturiano," August 24, 2007, www.youtube.com/watch?v=SVKKRzemX_w; and Mahalia Jackson with Nat Kong Cole, "Steal Away": "Steal Away - Mahalia Jackson & Nat King Cole from Emeless," YouTube video, 4:47, posted by "Emeless," November 29, 2006, www.youtube.com/watch?v=-O5hz5KnSdc.

He who disciplines the nations, does he not rebuke?
He who teaches man knowledge—
    the Lord—knows the thoughts of man,
    that they are but a breath.

Blessed is the man whom you discipline, O Lord,
    and whom you teach out of your law,
to give him rest from days of trouble,
    until a pit is dug for the wicked.
For the Lord will not forsake his people;
    he will not abandon his heritage;
for justice will return to the righteous,
    and all the upright in heart will follow it.

Who rises up for me against the wicked?
    Who stands up for me against evildoers?
If the Lord had not been my help,
    my soul would soon have lived in the land of silence.
When I thought, "My foot slips,"
    your steadfast love, O Lord, held me up.
When the cares of my heart are many,
    your consolations cheer my soul. (Ps 94:8-19)

One of the most powerful answers in a spiritual is found in "On Time God." The lines say it forcefully: "God don't come when you want him to, but he'll be there right on time."[16] Like the psalms, the range of biblical and theological content in spirituals is astonishing. Perhaps no other genre has been loved by so many, in no small part because spirituals address every human question.

---

[16]Listen to the Spiritual Union Mass Choir's version of it here: "'He's An On Time God' sung by the Spiritual Union Mass Choir," YouTube video, 5:32, posted by "Leroy Morgan," January 6, 2017, www.youtube.com/watch?v=OW7meP1BN5M. Dottie People's has made it her theme song: "Dottie Peoples - He's an on time God," YouTube video, 4:53, posted by "erastusbean," March 6, 2009, www.youtube.com/watch?v=mRgvYgOJK6g.

RIDING THE RAILS

Slaves occasionally did manage to find liberation by escaping. One of the ways was through a network of secret pathways and hidden shelters leading from the South either to northern states or to Canada. A good deal has been written about the Underground Railroad. Increasingly, historians and society at large are remembering leaders such as Harriet Tubman, the "Black Moses," who collected funds and met with sympathizers who could provide a safe harbor to escapees.[17] The people who helped the enslaved connect to the escape route were known as *agents* or *shepherds*. The guides were *conductors*. Hiding places were *stations*. The trains were known as *gospel trains*. A number of *station masters*, such as Black abolitionist William Still, hid scores of slaves in their homes until their release could be assured.[18] John Parker, a freed slave who eventually started a successful tobacco business, distinguished himself by leading hundreds of slaves across the Ohio River, at considerable risk to his own life, from Kentucky to Ripley, Ohio, and then on to the free states in the North.[19]

Spirituals were sometimes used by the shepherds. Employing the double meaning of spirituals, they could sing, "I'm on my way to Canaan Land," such that it was at one level about going to heaven. But Canaan was also a code word for Canada. Another example is "Follow the Drinking Gourd," a marvelous song ostensibly about fetching water, but also calling attention to the North Star (which was found at the pinnacle of the Big Dipper, like the shape of a gourd) and heading north to safety. Likewise, "Wade in the Water" was a spiritual about crossing the Jordan

---

[17]Excellent histories include William Still, *The Underground Railroad Records: Narrating the Hardships, Hairbreadth Escapes, and Death Struggles of Slaves in Their Efforts for Freedom* (New York: Modern Library, 2019); Colson Whitehead, *The Underground Railroad* (New York: Anchor, 2016); Kate Clifford Larson, *Bound for the Promised Land: Harriet Tubman: Portrait of an American Hero* (New York: One World, 2004); and the extraordinary children's book by Jacob Lawrence, *Harriet and the Promised Land* (New York: Simon & Schuster, 1993).

[18]William Still's chronicle of the underground railroad remains a valuable source of information about its operations. Still, *Underground Railroad Records*, 76-77.

[19]John P. Parker, *Promised Land: The Autobiography of John P. Parker, Former Slave and Conductor on the Underground Railroad* (New York: W. W. Norton, 1996).

Figure 6.1. Harriet Tubman, the "Moses" of the abolitionist movement, who organized the Underground Railroad

and receiving new life in Christ through baptism, but it also warned that if you were going to reach the "Promised Land," then you might need to go into the river so the slavecatcher's dogs lose the scent.

WORLD ACCLAIM

Spirituals have touched hundreds of millions of people down through the decades. An inspiring episode comes from the Fisk Jubilee Singers. Founded in 1866 in Nashville, Tennessee, Fisk University was the first university in America to accept students in liberal arts "irrespective of color." Partly for fundraising purposes, the savvy treasurer George L. White created a traveling singing group. Named for the biblical prophecy in Leviticus 25, the Jubilee Singers gained renown first in small towns but eventually all over the world. They were the subject of adulation, curiosity,

FISK JUBILEE SINGERS

Figure 6.2. The Fisk Jubilee Singers were among the first popularizers of spirituals.

and some criticism (partly because they did not perform in the vaudeville style of minstrels). In the lobby of the main building at the university are a series of paintings showing the Singers before Queen Victoria, visibly moved by the choir.[20]

Today, spirituals are beloved throughout the world and performed by a variety of singers, including White performers. But nothing matches the sincere execution of spirituals in the Black church by people whose lives have been defined by them.

[20]The entire history of the Singers is beautifully told by Andrew Ward, *Dark Midnight When I Rise: The Story of the Fisk Jubilee Singers* (New York: Amstad/Harper Collins, 2001). See also J. B. T. Marsh, *The Story of the Jubilee Singers with Songs* (London: Hodder and Stoughton, 1875), 69. Listen to an early recording (1909) of *Swing Low, Sweet Chariot*: "Swing Low Sweet Chariot - Fisk Jubilee Singers (1909)," YouTube video, 4:05, posted by "Nathaniel Jordon," December 23, 2012, www.youtube.com/watch?v=GUvBGZnL9rE. On the history of slave songs, including the Jubilee singers, see "The Story of the Jubilee Singers, Who Introduced the World to the Music of Black America (2000)," YouTube video, 1:07:44, posted by "Way Back," September 24, 2016, www.youtube.com/watch?v=dYwKkNXQ3SM.

7

PRECIOUS LORD

MOVING TO GOSPEL

When there's music in your soul, there's soul in your music.

CRISS JAMI

African American spirituals did not freeze into one timeless form. Like other genres or forms of music, they changed. A major shift occurred in the twentieth century, with a new style of music known as gospel coming into prominence. Today many know this music through popular films such as *Sister Act*, which gave the song "Oh Happy Day" notoriety. That particular song was originally performed by the Edwin Hawkins Singers, but today is sung by almost every church choir.[1]

Gospel titles have often been used without recognition of their provenance. For example, the title song of the coming-of-age film *Stand by Me*, often sung as a love ballad, is actually a gospel song written by the great composer Charles Albert Tindley. He based the song on Psalm 46:2: "Therefore we will not fear, Even though the earth be removed, And though the mountains be carried into the midst of the sea" (KJV). There are several versions of it. The 1986 film uses the rather easy-listening, pop version by Ben E. King. But it has also been rendered by John Lennon and

---

[1]Here's a version by the choir of the First Baptist Church of Glenarden: "'Oh Happy Day' Edwin Hawkins - Anthony Brown w/ FBCG Combined Choir," YouTube video, 6:35, posted by "Inside FBCG," February 14, 2018, www.youtube.com/watch?v=olQrCfkvbGw.

Bruce Springsteen, as well as the powerful version sung at Prince Harry and Meghan Markle's wedding in 2018.[2] But many people seem not to know the origins of gospel music.

Steve Turner, in his marvelous book *An Illustrated History of Gospel*, argues that whereas gospel is one of the main feeder genres into rock, jazz, and pop, it was often ignored or downplayed by people outside the church, possibly because many are hostile to the clear message of the songs about God's love and redemption through Jesus Christ.[3] I remember attending a Newport Folk Festival where a Black gospel singer rather naïvely (or was it?) told the mostly White audience all about sin and the love of God. There was a bewildered though respectful silence. The world of the church was just natural to him, yet it was so foreign to the audience.

Some Black musicians, while not altogether disapproving of gospel, feel that they are not as authentic as spirituals. They contend certain "secular" genres don't belong in the church. In one interview, soul singer Ray Charles told Turner, "I had something I wanted to do and I couldn't do what I wanted to do in the church. I wanted to play jazz music and you just don't play jazz music in church."[4] With the greatest respect, and indeed much love for Ray, whose view is shared by many, I will try to argue that the wall of separation need not be so high.

TAKE MY HAND

Like spirituals, gospel music grew out of the Black experience and the Black church. But if the spirituals tended to reflect misery and suffering, gospel music tended to emphasize the reality of joy, both of which were essential elements to jazz. Gospel was generally a more energetic music than spirituals, but not necessarily less Christ-centered. It was urban, not rural. There could be showmanship, but usually it was not over the top.

---

[2] "Stand by Me | Prince Harry and Meghan Markle exchange vows - The Royal Wedding - BBC," YouTube video, 8:16, posted by "BBC," May 19, 2018, www.youtube.com/watch?v=vZcQhZHr354.
[3] Steve Turner, *An Illustrated History of Gospel: Gospel Music from Early Spirituals to Contemporary Urban* (Oxford: Lion, 2010), 13-16.
[4] Turner, *Illustrated History*, 149. By "jazz" he would have included gospel.

Tony Heilbut, a defender of gospel, reminds us, "Singers today still live off the mannerisms developed by the gospel pioneers, just as rock bands echo the jazz and blues of thirty years ago."[5]

Gospel music did not just suddenly appear. It has somewhat complex origins. From time to time, the church has felt the need to make its singing more accessible to congregations. Isaac Watts (1674–1748) was a pioneer in reforming hymns, making them more Christ-centered and more singable. Among his best-known hymns are "When I Survey the Wondrous Cross" and "Our God Our Help in Ages Past." In the eighteenth century, John Newton ("Amazing Grace") and Augustus Toplady ("Rock of Ages") were notable modern hymn writers. The nineteenth century revival movements contributed significantly to singable hymns. Great musicians such as Ira Sankey, Philip Bliss, and Fanny Crosby wrote thousands of songs, many of which are still in the church's repertoire. Yet these modern hymns did not emerge unopposed, as many traditionalists defended the exclusivity of established psalm singing.[6]

While at its beginnings gospel music was not race-specific, the twentieth century saw increasing division along racial lines. For example, southern gospel is a genre that began in the early twentieth century. It was mostly sung by White people, though it was occasionally influenced by Black music. It was made popular by traveling singers and teachers, as well as radio, and the growing popularity of male quartets. Songs such as "Give the World a Smile" became best-sellers. More recently, Bill and Gloria Gaither embraced the southern gospel style and spread it through the *Gaither Homecoming* tours and videos. Other subgenres such as Christian Country Music (Inspirational Country), which features well-known singers like Larry Gaitlan and Charlie Daniels, can be traced to the southern gospel tradition.

---

[5]Tony Heilbut, *The Gospel Sound: Good News and Bad Times* (New York: Simon & Schuster, 1972), 30.

[6]See, for example, *Singing the Lord's Song in a Strange Land: Hymnody in the History of North American Protestantism*, eds. Edith L. Blumhofer and Mark A. Noll (Tuscaloosa: University of Alabama Press, 2004); and Millar Patrick, *The Story of the Church's Song* (Claremont, CA: Pomona, 2008).

Beginning in the 1920s, Black gospel music emerged more resolutely. There were many varieties of Black gospel: soloists, small choirs, mass choirs, and gospel quartets. And there were many venues: churches, records, radio, concerts, and public demonstrations. Besides superstars like Mahalia Jackson (1911–1972), who is probably the best-known gospel singer, one of the most significant figures was Thomas Andrew Dorsey (1899–1993). His story took him from rural Georgia, where he was an accomplished blues musician, to Chicago and the mainstream gospel movement.[7] His father was a minister, and his mother was a pianist. While he went away from the church for a while, he came back, partly through the preaching and singing of "Professor" W. M. Nix. The song that drew him in was "I Do, Don't You?" Most of his life he believed the blues and gospel were, if not the same thing, close cousins. Blues, jazz, and gospel were "vehicles for our feeling."[8] Yet, he eventually went full time into composing and singing gospel in order to "serve the Lord."[9]

Dorsey came along at the lowest point of the Great Depression, and his music livened-up and enriched the churches.[10] His best-known song is "Take My Hand, Precious Lord." It was reportedly Martin Luther King Jr.'s favorite song. It was composed right after the deaths of Dorsey's first wife and a child. Closely bound to a song by George Nelson Allen, Dorsey's tune was more of a melodic oration. Its simplicity is compelling:

Precious Lord take my hand,

Lead me on, let me stand,

I am tired, I am weak, I am worn.

Through the storm, through the night,

Lead me on to the light,

Take my hand precious Lord, lead me on.[11]

---

[7]His story is beautifully told by Michael W. Harris, *The Rise of Gospel Blues: The Music of Thomas Andrew Dorsey in the Urban Church* (New York: Oxford University Press, 1992).

[8]Harris, *Rise of Gospel Blues*, 97.

[9]Harris, *Rise of Gospel Blues*, 98.

[10]Heilbut, *Gospel Sound*, 65.

[11]Many versions exist. We possess several recordings of Dorsey himself singing it: "Thomas Dorsey-Take My Hand, Precious Lord," YouTube video, 4:24, posted by "Walter Robinson,"

Different, on the surface, from solo gospel music are the quartets, usually an all-male group, often literally with four vocalists, but that number could increase to five or six or seven. They sang close harmony, using newer gospel tunes as well as older spirituals. Each city had its own major gospel quartets, but perhaps Memphis, Tennessee, was the greatest hub. The Spirit of Memphis Quartet, a group that combined the pain of suffering with hope in the good news, was the quintessence of great singing.[12]

TO THE STAGE

Though the golden age of gospel (1945–1960) has passed by, a number of present-day gospel choirs and smaller groups remain active. The music has never been more popular in Europe. Gospel jazz ensembles are well liked today. One of the most notable is the Grammy-winning *Take 6*, an extraordinary a cappella men's group that combines jazz with spirituals. Their close harmonies and compelling rhythms have attracted many leading performers today with whom they often collaborate.[13]

August 4, 2013, www.youtube.com/watch?v=4HNZNvlhlN4. Listen to the moving rendition by Mahalia Jackson: "MAHALIA JACKSON PRECIOUS LORD TAKE MY HAND," YouTube video, 5:03, posted by "Thejazzsingers channel," June 18, 2009, www.youtube.com/watch?v=as1rsZenwNc. Equally inspirational is Fantasia singing it at Aretha Franklin's funeral, blending it into "You've Got a Friend in Jesus": "Fantasia Sings 'Precious Lord Take My Hand' At Funeral Of Aretha Franklin," YouTube video, 5:35, posted by "Lauren JNel," August 31, 2018, www.youtube.com/watch?v=Ay2Fi_Ao_tU. Elvis Presley's version is sweet and compelling in its own way: "Take My Hand, Precious Lord - Elvis Presley," YouTube video, 3:19, posted by "maria mountain824," August 17, 2015, www.youtube.com/watch?v=ThsYX4RBtbw.

[12]We are fortunate to possess some of their recordings at their best. See "Spirit of Memphis Quartet - He Never Left Me Alone," YouTube video, 2:46, posted by "poachedeyes," July 23, 2008, www.youtube.com/watch?v=ta7cVlqJK_4. Unafraid to sing of the full range of Christian doctrine, here they are singing about judgment: "SPIRIT OF MEMPHIS QUARTET - Sign of the Judgement," YouTube video, 2:59, posted by "gollincho," January 25, 2009, www.youtube.com/watch?v=8sT3f_cFo4A. And there is the great classic "Ease My Trouble and Mind": "The Spirit of Memphis Quartet - Ease My Trouble In Mind," YouTube video, 2:32, posted by "Sliptrail," July 31, 2016, www.youtube.com/watch?v=Ex1WMFBLviY.

[13]For a sample, listen to "take 6 - If We Ever Needed the Lord Before (We Sure Do Need Him Now)," YouTube video, 5:02, posted by "katherinnnnne," March 17, 2012, www.youtube.com/watch?v=i_avcdMEeCs.

Broadway shows are occasionally produced that are gospel-based. *Your Arms Too Short to Box with God* is an outstanding rendition of a theme suggested by James Weldon Johnson's *Autobiography of an Ex-Colored Man*. Though ultimately derived from Isaiah 59:1, which reads "Surely the arm of the Lord is not too short to save," Weldon's poem, nestled in the novel, says, "Young man, Young man, your arm's too short to box with God" and goes on to say everyone, including the two sons in the parable of the prodigal son, is guilty of expecting too much from God's power on their own terms. The music by Alex Bradford is infused with gospel. Many other examples exist.

The borders between musical genres, including the spirituals and gospel, are rarely completely clear. It may be easier to say that spirituals are older and more conservative, while gospel is more modern and decidedly urban. If spirituals are more associated with the church, then gospel music is capable of adaptation to the world outside the church. Generally speaking, it is less sorrowful than spirituals, and it more clearly expresses joy, but of course there are exceptions. Most of the best singers and ensembles combined high-quality music with a zeal for evangelism. Despite a low profile, gospel has been successfully incorporated into the music of public performers. And, like the spirituals, gospel significantly shaped the music of jazz.

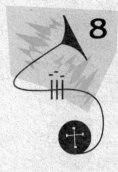

8

WOKE UP
THIS MORNING

THE BLUES

The personalized, solo elements of the blues style may indicate

a decisive move into a twentieth-century American consciousness,

but the musical style of the blues indicates a holding on to the old

roots at the very time when the dispersion of the Negroes throughout

the country and the rise of the radio and the phonograph could have

spelled the demise of a distinctive Afro-American musical style.

LAWRENCE W. LEVINE

The blues! There has perhaps never been such powerful, simple folk music that comments so effectively on everyday life. They are not synonymous with jazz, but jazz makes no sense without them. What is their aesthetic? Listening to Little Walter singing *My Babe* will help you understand, as its themes of faithlessness and loss could not be more obvious.[1]

My baby don't stand no cheatin', my babe

Oh yeah she don't stand no cheatin', my babe

---

[1] "Little Walter My Babe," YouTube, 2:34, posted by "Angel Neira," April 11, 2009, www.youtube.com/watch?v=duRp_avXtMM.

Oh yeah she don't stand no cheatin',

She don't stand none of that midnight creepin'

My babe, tiny little baby, my babe.

And the harmony could not be simpler. There are only three chords, what musicians call the tonic, the subdominant, the dominant. In fact, this progression is nearly universal in Western music, from Beethoven's *Moonlight Sonata* to the first prelude in Bach's *Well-Tempered Clavier*. It also shows up in rock, which is the direct heir to the blues through "rhythm and blues."[2] But what particularly distinguishes the blues musically is the passionate way the notes are bent as the voice reflects the harmonica and the guitar.

The lyrics are often a multilayered reflection on faithfulness in the face of temptation. The song is multilayered because on the surface there is an appreciation for the faithful relationship between a man and a woman. At a deeper level, as we shall see, is the echo of a moral framework in which cheating, whether in relationships or with God, is frowned upon. And at the deepest level, the blues are a *theodicy*, raising the question of God's goodness in the face of pervasive evil. And that is perhaps their greatest contribution to jazz.

This is why lost love is characteristic of many blues songs. There are different levels to abandonment in these songs. Of course, in real life, such losses happen: our baby, our love, boyfriend or girlfriend, husband or wife, does leave sometimes. But, at a deeper level, they are a commentary on alienation. In slavery, the colonist would steal the laborer only to abandon him or her to the wiles of a foreign country where they were never welcomed in the first place. If betrayal and abandonment are often the subject of the blues, they are not without hope. That hope may not be stated in so many words, but it is there, in part just in the fact that one can sing at all.

The oft-recorded *Saint Louis Blues* is a classic blues song. It is a lament by a woman over a man who left her for someone else:

---

[2]A popular saying, attributed to blues singer Muddy Waters, is that "the blues had a baby and they named it rock 'n' roll."

I hate to see that evening sun go down

Oh, I hate to see that evening sun go down

Because my baby he done left this town

In the subsequent lyrics, the cheating man went after a woman with diamond rings and store-bought hair who drags him around by her apron strings. Yet, even amid such loss, the song overall is neither nihilistic nor despairing.[3]

A comparison may help us better understand the uniqueness of the blues. Think of the nineteenth-century *lieder* of Franz Schubert. Here is one from his anthology *Wintereise* where the poet recounts a failed relationship:

A stranger I arrived here,

a stranger I go hence.

Maytime was good to me

with many a bunch of flowers.

The girl spoke of love,

her mother even of marriage.

Now the world is dismal,

the path veiled in snow.

There is a deep lovelorn sorrow here, but how different it is from the raw sorrow, the umbrage of Joe Thomas's blues in *My Baby's Done Left Me*:

My baby's done left me,

And I'm about to lose my mind

My baby's done left me,

---

[3]One may sample a wonderful version of this classic by Bessie Smith, with Louis Armstrong on cornet: "Bessie Smith - St. Louis Blues, 1925," YouTube video, 3:15, posted by "240252," March 24, 2012, www.youtube.com/watch?v=3rd9IaA_uJI.

And I'm about to lose my mind

I just can't get nobody else

'Cause you know love is a doggon lie[4]

ORIGINS

The blues are a natural outgrowth of the work songs and "sorrow songs" that developed on slave plantations. Historically, the blues came into their own during Reconstruction. The temporary exhilaration of emancipation was indeed both elating and deeply disappointing. Among the reasons are the tenacious ways after the war that the plantation owners tried to hold on to the older economy, so dependent as it was on human laborers.

But the main reason was entrenched racism. Whereas much could have been accomplished if only voters' rights had been ensured, a number of strategies were devised to prevent the franchise from being accessed by Black people. In order to justify this, a narrative was developed that could convince the already willing minds of the traditionalists. Perhaps the most compelling of these was created by Edward A. Pollard, journalist for the *Richmond Examiner*. Just a year after the end of the Civil War he wrote about the "Lost Cause," which he claimed was a "New Southern History of the War of the Confederates."[5] In his account, though the South must submit to the restoration of the Union and the end of slavery, that did not have to mean racial equality. His was a defense of White supremacy, one that has had great tenacity over the years, right down to the present day. It was more than just raw hatred, though there was plenty of that. It was a battle for ideas, he claimed.

Perhaps the most articulate commentator for freedom and justice was Frederick Douglass. Like Pollard, Douglass thought it was a battle of ideas. But very much unlike him, he saw the battle as between

---

[4]"Joe Thomas - My Baby Done Left Me (1949)," YouTube video, 2:48, posted by "Overjazz," October 7, 2012, www.youtube.com/watch?v=x7BMImgCjNc.

[5]See David Blight, *Race and Reunion: The Civil War in American Memory* (Cambridge, MA: Harvard University Press, 2001), 2.

slavery and freedom, barbarism and civilization. Henry Louis Gates captures some of the exhilaration, followed by the bitter disappointment of the decades following the war, in his study *Stony the Road*.[6] He credits Douglass with advocating two nonnegotiables in order for Reconstruction to be guaranteed: education (90 percent of freed Black people were illiterate after the war) and the vote. Both were met with enormous obstacles.

Thus, the joy of emancipation was followed not with a gradual liberation of the oppressed, but with harsh new measures of repression. This era, known as Jim Crow, lasted at least until the civil rights movement of the 1950s and 1960s.[7] It is the era in which the blues were born, though surely the roots go back further, possibly even to Africa.[8]

THE MYTHOLOGY OF THE BLUES

The blues are ensconced in mythology. Take, for example, one of the prevailing stories about one of the most admired but least well-documented blues singers, Robert Johnson. Though we have very few recordings of Johnson, the ones we have are prized collectors' items. The story goes that Robert Johnson made a bargain with the devil that had the effect of enhancing his music but alienating him from the church and from more conservative audiences. He supposedly met the devil at a crossroad. Indeed, a number of Johnson's songs refer to roads and intersections. In the original title he asks the Lord to help him out of his lostness. The "Crossroad Blues" (1936) says it clearly:

---

[6]Henry Louis Gates Jr., *Stony the Road: Reconstruction, White Supremacy, and the Rise of Jim Crow* (New York: Penguin Books, 2019), 20-38.

[7]Named after a character made popular by Thomas Dartmouth Rice (1808–1860), who painted his face black and performed in vaudeville acts centering on this dubious character. For a sobering account, see "What Was Jim Crow," Jim Crow Museum of Racist Memorabilia at Ferris State University, www.ferris.edu/jimcrow/what.htm.

[8]For just some of the histories of blues, see James H. Cone, *The Spirituals and the Blues* (Maryknoll, NY: Orbis, 1972); Stephen J. Nichols, *Getting the Blues: What Blues Music Teaches Us About Suffering and Salvation* (Grand Rapids, MI: Brazos, 2008); Ted Gioia, *Delta Blues: The Life and Times of the Mississippi Masters Who Revolutionized American Music* (New York: W. W. Norton, 2008); Giles Oakley, *The Devil's Music: A History of the Blues* (Boston: Da Capo, 1997).

I went to the crossroad,

Fell down on my knee

I went to the crossroad,

Fell down on my knee

Have mercy, now save poor Bob

If you please.[9]

The lyrics to one of his most powerful songs, "Cool Drink of Water Blues," contain these lines:

Crying, I ain't going down this big road by myself,

Why don't you hear me talking pretty mama,

Lord, ain't going down this big road by myself.

If I don't carry you, [you're] going to carry someone else.[10]

Where does this story come from? Skeptics aver that it was made up or perpetuated by Johnson himself. However, it is not wise to deny the likelihood of some sort of credible background for the story. Ted Gioia argues that the story of the devil at the crossroads has African origins but has been transferred to the racial oppression of Black people in North America. The devil here vaguely resembles the trickster figure we have met who is able to outwit the oppressors. Gioia concludes, "The Devil, as a sign of evil, couldn't help but conjure up a sympathetic feeling among those listeners who felt that as African Americans in a White world, they needed an *agent of opposition* to carry on through their lives."[11]

---

[9]"Robert Johnson- Crossroad," YouTube video, 2:48, posted by "shogun coredump," April 13, 2007, www.youtube.com/watch?v=Yd60nI4sa9A

[10]Cited in Ted Gioia, *Delta Blues*, 119. Here is a version by Tommy Johnson (no relation): "Cool Drink Of Water Blues - TOMMY JOHNSON (1928) Delta Blues Guitar Legend," YouTube video, 3:27, posted by "RagtimeDorianHenry," April 5, 2009, www.youtube.com /watch?v=o808EmOukDQ.

[11]Gioia, *Delta Blues*, 164-65.

SACRED AND SECULAR

This raises one of the most significant issues related to the blues. Are they an entirely secular genre, referring only to broken relationships? Or is there more to it than that?

Amiri Baraka (formerly known as Leroi Jones) argues that the blues are resolutely anti-White and thoroughly secular.[12] One should understand that Baraka was a founding member of the Black Arts Group and identified with much of Black Power's opposition to the White establishment as the movement saw it. He eventually embraced international Marxism and wrote against bourgeois culture.[13] His assessment of the blues is nevertheless rich and informative. And he is right to an extent: there certainly is a *protest* embedded in the blues, as is the case of jazz.

James Cone, who has written on the blues as well as spirituals, argues that although the blues depict the "secular" dimension of Black experience, they are not divorced from theological considerations. The difference with spirituals is only the setting: one is for church, relating directly to God and his people, and the other observes all of life, mostly outside the church. He argues that standard categories of White theology often lack the realism to deal with life's hardships. Here is how he puts it, partly quoting the scholar Sterling Brown:

> [The Blues] express the "laments of folk Negroes over hard luck, careless or unrequited love, broken family life, or general dissatisfaction with a cold and trouble-filled world." And implied in the Blues is a stubborn refusal to go beyond the existential problem and substitute otherworldly answers. It is not that the Blues reject God; rather they *ignore* God by embracing the joys and sorrows of life, such as those of a man's relationship with his woman, a woman with her man.[14]

---

[12]Amiri Baraka, *Negro People in White America* (London: MacGibbon and Kee, 1965).
[13]See his *Transbluesency: The Selected Poetry of Amiri Baraka/LeRoi Jones* (1961–1995) (Venice: Marsilio, 1995).
[14]The embedded quote is from Sterling Brown, *The Negro Caravan* (New York: Arno, 1972), 426. The rest of the quote is from Cone, *Spirituals and the Blues*, 99. Italics original.

The word *ignore* here is too strong in my judgment. I believe he recognizes this because he proceeds to say that the blues are "secular spirituals" and only secular in the sense that the main subject matter is everyday life and often related to the human body. In my own outlook the term *secular* is ill-chosen. As one of my mentors put it, "There is no proper sacred-secular distinction, because everything is sacred."[15] That is, everything somehow belongs to God.

Blues guitarist John Cephas agrees and puts it more positively:

People may tell you there is a big difference between religious songs and the blues because the people in the church don't hold to you singing about anything other than your relationship with God. But I don't think God intended for it to be like that. He gave us music. He gave us the knowledge to express ourselves in song. He gave us these instruments; he gave us everything. So, where's the difference between expressing your relationship with him and singing about your relationship to something else in your life?[16]

Ethnomusicologist Jon Michael Spencer goes deeper. In his extraordinary study, *Blues and Evil*, he argues that the blues are profoundly religious, even Christian, although not directly. The blues are not strictly worship music, yet they make no sense apart from a theistic worldview. Embedded in the blues, he notes, are a number of minor clues to their Christian background. Phrases such as "Lord, Lord," "Oh Lord," "Lord have mercy," and the like punctuate the lyrics. These are not simply random interpolations but derive from the church background most blues singers come from, reflecting a sincere belief in God.[17]

More importantly, the larger picture includes the main elements of Christian theology put into poetry. There is the recognition of the fall of humanity and the pervasiveness of sin. In the blues, we find a highly

---

[15]Pierre Courthial, emeritus dean of the Reformed Seminary in Aix-en-Provence, France, in personal conversation.

[16]John Cephas, "The Blues," in *The Blues Aesthetic: Black Culture and Modernism* (Washington, DC: Washington Project for the Arts, 1989), 15.

[17]Jon Michael Spencer, *Blues and Evil* (Knoxville: University of Tennessee Press, 1993), 37-38.

developed awareness of sin and the tension between transgression and desire for the virtuous. For example, in "Half of Me Wants to Be Good," the wonderful singer Ethel Waters reflects the struggle Paul articulated in Romans 7. The blues singer is often a *prodigal* as in Jesus' parable in Luke 15. This might mean simple repentance. Robert Wilkins, for example, played the blues in Memphis in 1915 with such greats as Charlie Patton and Son House. But he felt guilty as he raised his children and came back to the church in 1950, becoming ordained in the Church of God in Christ.[18] One of my favorite singers is (the Rev.) Blind Gary Davis (1896–1972).[19] An abused child, he ended up performing blues and gospel in Durham, North Carolina, in 1920. He then had a dramatic conversion to Christ and was ordained a Baptist minister in 1933. From then on, he sang only Christian songs until his death.[20] No doubt, like Ray Charles, he erected a high wall between the sacred and the secular.

Sometimes the blues singer turned not only into a Christian person but into a preacher.[21] Son House's masterpiece, "Preachin' the Blues," illustrates such songs. The piece was likely a version of the amazing Bessie Smith's song of the same title recorded in 1927, though she used a piano accompaniment rather than a guitar. It was said of Bessie Smith that for her, blues and worship were inseparable. "That's why her blues seemed almost like hymns."[22] Her wall was low!

I have come to believe there are strong parallels between the blues and the Wisdom literature of the Bible. Hebrew poetry is based in part on *parallelism*. For example, here are some words from Habakkuk 1:2:

> O Lord, how long shall I cry for help,
>   and you will not hear?

18Spencer, *Blues and Evil*, 65.

19See Ian Zack, *Say No to the Devil: The Life and Genius of Rev. Gary Davis* (Chicago: University of Chicago Press, 2015). He tells his own story in "Blind Gary Davis (1964)," YouTube video, 10:35, posted by "A/V Geeks," August 15, 2012, www.youtube.com/watch?v=lQrJvWHrFTc.

20See Rev. Blind Gary Davis, *Complete Recorded Works, 1935–1949* (Document Records DOCD-5060).

21Daniel Beaumont, *Preachin' the Blues: The Life and Times of Son House* (New York: Oxford University Press, 2011).

22Chris Albertson, *Bessie* (New Haven, CT: Yale University Press, 2003), 130.

Or cry to you "Violence!"
    and you will not save?

These could be blues lyrics! Blues poetry employs parallelism as well. Blues singers in the Bible would have to include Job, Qoheleth, the psalmist, and of course Jesus himself. When he cried out to God in the Garden of Gethsemane, "My Father, if it be possible, let this cup pass from me" (Mt 26:39), it could be considered a blues prayer![23]

JUDGMENT

Another feature of the blues which echoes a biblical worldview is *reckoning*. The ethic of "you reap what you sow" is often woven into the fabric of blues lyrics. Consider the popular "Gypsy Woman" by Muddy Waters:

> You know the gypsy woman told me that your mother's bad luck child
>
> You know the gypsy woman told me that your mother's bad luck child
>
> Well, you're having a good time now, but that'll be trouble after a while.[24]

In his marvelous song titled, "Key to the Highway," Big Bill Broonzy sees himself riding into the West Texas sunset:

> Come here, sweet mama, now and help me with this heavy load
>
> I am due in West Texas, and I've got to get on the road
>
> I'm goin' to West Texas, I'm goin' down beyond the farm
>
> I'm gonna ask the good Lord what evil I have done[25]

---

[23]See Ruth Naomi Floyd, "Blues," in *It Was Good: Art to the Glory of God*, ed. Ned Bustard (Baltimore, MD: Square Halo, 2013), 191-98.

[24]"Muddy Waters - Gypsy Woman (1948)," YouTube video, 2:35, posted by "77GhettoD," March 31, 2011, www.youtube.com/watch?v=L8v3jtL1S6k.

[25]"Big Bill Broonzy - Key to the Highway," YouTube video, 3:02, posted by "KouKlouvahata Puppet Theatre," February 17, 2011, www.youtube.com/watch?v=KN_f0WVsHuw.

Spencer calls this a *theodicy* in the blues.[26] This technical term was coined by the philosopher Leibniz in order to find a way to justify the goodness of God in the face of evil. Though there are plenty of blues reflecting the "reap-what-you-sow" view, Spencer and Anthony Pinn would tell us not to ignore those that simply ask the question without giving an answer.[27]

We are fortunate today to possess all kinds of testaments making the blues accessible. The most appealing, of course, is the live performance. Though many of the legends have passed on, some are still with us. A visit to the Chicago Loop will repay any effort to spend time there. Some of the blues clubs feature relatively unknown though talented musicians. Some of the great stars are alive and well and giving regular performances, including Buddy Guy (b. 1936), who embodies the high-powered urban blues of the previous century. The list of musicians he has inspired is like a who's who of fabled performers, including Eric Clapton, Jimi Hendrix, and many others.[28]

Thanks to documentaries and recordings, we have access to many of the greats who have shaped blues history. Mention must be made of B. B. King, whose subtle guitar style introduced a rare level of sophistication to the music. Like so many, King started his love of music in the church; he sang regularly in gospel choirs. His signature song, "The Thrill Is Gone," moves any listener, whether adept at the blues or not. Other greats include Muddy Waters, John Lee Hooker, Lightning Hopkins, Mississippi John Hurt, Junior Wells, Elmore James, and countless others.[29]

For those interested in the rural blues, tastefully done tours sponsored by the Mississippi Delta Tourism Association in Clarksdale take the

---

[26]Spencer, *Blues and Evil*, 78.

[27]See Anthony B. Pinn, *Why, Lord? Suffering and Evil in Black Theology* (New York: Continuum, 1999).

[28]Buddy Guy with David Ritz, *When I Left Home: My Story* (Philadelphia: Da Capo, 2012) is an invaluable source of firsthand witnesses to the great moments in blues performances.

[29]Many excellent histories of the blues exist. For example, see Robert Palmer, *Deep Blues* (New York: Penguin, 1981) and Giles Oakley, *The Devil's Music* (New York: Da Capo, 1997). For an unusual yet deeply moving account, see Langston Hughes, *The Weary Blues* (New York: Knopf, 2015).

visitor down the "Blues Trail." It takes you to various markers, grave sites, old cabins, and the Delta Blues Museum. There you can feast on the memories of Charlie Patton, Son House, and of course the matchless Robert Johnson.

Like gospel, and for many of the same reasons, the blues have a nearly universal appeal. My own band has performed in former communist countries, particularly in Eastern Europe. Inevitably, when we render a blues number, the room is silent, and people are often moved to tears. Understandably, some people balk at the rawness, even at times the gratuitous sex and violence in the blues. To those who are unable to discern anything deeper, I say, ignore these songs. But just don't throw out the baby with the bathwater! The blues address the full range of the human experience, so we should expect to find love and loss, pain and joy, life and death. The serious questions posed—and some of the answers, even if tentative, offered—by the blues deeply shaped the development of jazz as both a musical genre and a theological statement.

PART III

JAZZ MUSIC

9

A WAY OF LIFE

HOW JAZZ CAME INTO BEING

One searches in vain through all the countries of the world
to find another example of such a rapid and dramatic
transformation from folk music to art music.

TED GIOIA

Having discussed at some length the various musical genres that informed the birth of jazz, we turn finally to jazz itself. As was the case with Renaissance art, impressionism, and the flourishing of early cinema, jazz is something of a miracle. Somehow, from all the roots we have examined, everything came together at the beginning of the twentieth century. The tributaries flowed into a central stream. The spirituals and the blues, theater and vaudeville, dancing and shouting, African American preaching and other popular oral styles, and even the "funeral with music" of the marching band—all of these and more fed into the river of jazz.

RAGTIME

We have made passing allusions to ragtime, but because it is nearly synonymous with jazz, special mention must be made. The word was the first used for what became jazz. It was a general kind of rhythmical music, one with plenty of swing, one characteristic of several genres. Yet a distinct use of the term was the popular piano style, played by traveling pianists who mostly converged in Missouri. It eventually was widely distributed through piano rolls. Piano ragtime was quite technically demanding. One of its characteristics is having a form close to the sonata, and yet using a good deal of syncopation: placing the down beat where you don't expect it. It was often characterized by sheer endurance. The story goes that one bystander stood outside a café where there was nonstop piano from dusk to dawn. When curiosity got the better of him, he walked in only to discover that the pianist played for ten minutes with his right hand, and then the next ten with his left, and on through the night.[1]

No one is altogether certain how this music emerged or why it suddenly became so popular. It may have originated with the banjo, followed by pianos imitating the banjo sound. One reason for its popularity is that it was played in St. Louis, a crossroads for travel—north and south, east and west. Travelers needed entertainment that was accessible, yet creative. It often gets revived, as it did with the smash-hit movie *The Sting*, starring Paul Newman and Robert Redford. After it came, every music student wanted to learn "The Entertainer," a simple, elegant tune in the dance tempo called the "two-step" popular at the turn of the century.[2]

Like jazz, piano ragtime evolved from being simply amusing entertainment to a true art form. By the time of the great composer Scott Joplin, the music was imaginative and deep. Joplin's "Maple Leaf Rag" is perhaps the best-known ragtime composition, the sheet music for which was published in 1899.[3] Joplin even wrote a ragtime opera, called *Treemonisha*, based on the story of a child found under a tree and subject to all the superstitious temptations of post–Civil War opportunity. In the end, only education is considered the true answer for life in the early twentieth

---

[1] See Tom Turpin, *The Ragtime Nightmare* (St Louis: Robert De Young, 1900).

[2] You may hear it in many versions. Joshua Rifkin's is the most artistically satisfying in my view: "Scott Joplin: The Entertainer & Ragtime Dance - Joshua Rifkin, Piano," YouTube video, 8:30, posted by "Audio Video," January 3, 2018, www.youtube.com/watch?v=q5ooh1YAnS0.

[3] Listen to this version by Joshua Rifkin, who plays it in the original, calm, almost "Mozartean" style: "Maple Leaf Rag," YouTube video, 3:20, posted by "Joshua Rifkin – Topic," November 8, 2014, www.youtube.com/watch?v=Rad6UvoGHV8.

century. The opera combines elements of ragtime, blues, and band music. Though rejected at the time, it has now been revived and performed on and off Broadway.[4]

By the 1920s, though ragtime was still played, much of it morphed into stride piano, which was largely based on the East Coast, particularly New York. It was played by marvelous artists like James P. Johnson, Fats Waller, and Lucky Roberts. But perhaps the greatest stride performer was Art Tatum, whose dazzling technique was coupled with astonishing chord construction.[5]

Figure 9.1. Art Tatum, considered by some to be the greatest jazz pianist of them all

[4]See Act 1 on video: "Treemonisha (part 1)," YouTube video, 25:43, posted by "Karl Skellenger," January 22, 2015, www.youtube.com/watch?v=b6ynOUAFIG8.

[5]"Art Tatum – Yesterdays," YouTube video, 2:00, posted by "eccentricXXX," September 6, 2008, www.youtube.com/watch?v=D9Cs_zb4ql4.

NEW ORLEANS

Though one could find a few significant developments elsewhere, the epi-center for the birth of jazz was undoubtedly the city of New Orleans. To the visitor from the outside, New Orleans is an exotic, colorful paradise of music and spicy cooking. A. J. Liebling compared it to a Mediterranean port transplanted to the Gulf of Mexico. Much of those impressions, though, are a veneer. Walker Percy, who lived and died in New Orleans, had a more clearheaded outlook. In *The Moviegoer*, he writes: "I alight in the Esplanade in a smell of roasting coffee and creosote and walk up Royal Street. The Lower Quarter is the best part. The ironwork on the balconies sags like rotten lace. Little French cottages hide behind high walls. Through deep sweating carriageways one catches glimpses of courtyards gone to jungle."[6]

New Orleans is easy to romanticize. To be sure, there are magical fea-tures to the city. Strolling around the French Quarter, with its art galleries and restaurants, honeymooners find an ideal location. But the city had been a major port in the slave trade, from which it profited. By the late nineteenth century, however, this once wealthy trading hub had become a pale shadow of itself. In 1878, 2 percent of the city died in a terrible yellow fever epidemic. Being on the gulf, and being late in developing a modern sewage system, disease was a constant threat. The life expectancy of a Black native of the city in 1880 was thirty-six years (White people usually lived ten more years). No wonder the funeral parade was a major part of life.

The traditional view is that jazz was born in the red-light district (Storyville) and much of it in brothels. Yet more recent research calls this account into question. Generally, the musicians did not want to play in bordellos or seedy places.[7] There were numerous places where jazz first appeared, including beachfront parties, Saturday night fish fries, funerals, service organizations, and the church.

---

[6]Quoted in Frank de Caro, ed., *Louisiana Sojourns: Travelers' Tales and Literary Journeys* (Baton Rouge: Louisiana State University Press, 1998), 104.

[7]A fine account of the relation of jazz to the city of New Orleans is by Ted Gioia, *The History of Jazz* (New York: Oxford University Press, 1997), 28-53. See also Teachout, *Pops*, 23-50.

EARLY PATTERNS

How did all of the music we have looked at, within all of the circumstances leading up to the twentieth century, become *jazz*? And how does it articulate the journey from deep misery to inextinguishable joy?

We see both of these emphases in the songs that led up to the birth of jazz. For example, the great spiritual "I'm So Glad Jesus Lifted Me" expresses both misery and joy:

I'm so glad Jesus lifted me.

I'm so glad Jesus lifted me.

I'm so glad Jesus lifted me,

singin' Glory, Hallelujah, Jesus lifted me!

When I was in trouble, Jesus lifted me.

When I was in trouble, Jesus lifted me.

When I was in trouble, Jesus lifted me,

singin' Glory, Hallelujah, Jesus lifted me![8]

Of course, some songs major on the suffering. Take the very moving spiritual "The Blind Man Stood by the Road and He Cried":

The blind man stood by the road and he cried

The blind man stood by the road and he cried

The blind man stood by the road and he cried

He cried oh, oh, oh

The woman stood by the well and she cried

The woman stood by the well and she cried

The woman stood by the well and she cried

---

[8]Listen to the version by Knee-C: "I'm So Glad Jesus Lifted Me," YouTube video, 4:27, posted by "Knee-C – Topic," May 21, 2015, www.youtube.com/watch?v=5-qRz8uEz3s.

She cried oh, oh, oh

Show me the way

Show me the way

Show me the way

The way to go home

Jesus hung from the cross and He cried

Jesus hung from the cross and He cried

Jesus hung from the cross and He cried

He cried oh, oh, oh

Show me the way

Show me the way

Show me the way

The way to go home.[9]

Meanwhile, some songs are almost completely joyful. Think of the marvelous "Fare Ye Well," otherwise known as "In That Great Getting Up Morning":

Well, in that great gettin' up mornin'

(Fare ye well, fare ye well)

Lord, in that great gettin' up mornin'

(Fare ye well, fare ye well)

Well, in that great gettin' up mornin'

(Fare ye well, fare ye well)

---

[9]There is a moving version of this sung by Josh White, with slightly different lyrics: "Blind Man Stood on the Road and Cried," YouTube video, 4:15, posted by "Josh White – Topic," December 25, 2014, www.youtube.com/watch?v=DAS6JjarxvM.

Well, in that great gettin' up mornin'

(Fare ye well, fare ye well)

Let me tell ya 'bout the comin' of judgment

(Fare ye well, fare ye well)

Let me tell ya 'bout the comin' of judgment

(Fare ye well, fare ye well)[10]

We may never know altogether just how these genres blended together, but come together they did to produce an enduring music. Pride of place, as we noted previously, must go first to the military band. And though various locations saw the rise of these bands, again, New Orleans was the mother abode. These groups played hymns and spirituals, albeit with a certain swing. The marching parades were freestyle, either joyful or mournful with a degree of improvisation. A good deal of music throughout history is improvisational, or at least full of ad-libbing. In classical music it abounds. Bach's "Royal Theme," used in the *Musical Offering*, for example, became the basis for a series of improvised variations. Entire movements in the great symphonies could be based on a theme, developed in scores of ways. Jazz, more than most Western music of the early twentieth century, made use of many variants possible within the set form of a piece. The sounds were bluesy. Notes were stretched and rendered passionately.

Thus, theme and variation are at the heart of jazz. To get the idea, consider the well-known standard "Ain't Misbehavin'," originally composed by Fats Waller. Listen to the composer rendering it on piano,[11] then

---

[10]No one sings this song better than Mahalia Jackson: "MAHALIA JACKSON – Great Gettin Up Morning," YouTube video, 7:24, posted by "jahboyz3," January 27, 2008, www.youtube .com/watch?v=zQgAQF0js1E. Steven Albertin notes the irony in some of the Black songs of joy, since they were created in the most wretched circumstances. Belief in the resurrection, Albertin argues, transcended the despicable conditions of slave life: Steven E. Albertin, *Through Cross-Colored Glasses* (Lima, OH: CSS, 2003).

[11]His own version can be heard here: "Fats Waller - Ain't Misbehavin' - Stormy Weather (1943)," YouTube video, 2:46, posted by "bessjazz," November 6, 2009, www.youtube.com /watch?v=PSNPpssruFY. From the film *Stormy Weather*, this version showcases the

listen to the marvelously varied version for solo guitar by Joe Pass.[12] Never within the dazzling array of chords, blue notes, and swing do we lose a sense of the original tune. As mentioned in the introduction, unless it is the blues, typically, standards follow the AABA format, the main melody repeated and then the bridge, with its contrasting material, then back to the top. This remarkably simple structure allows for all kinds of creative music-making.[13]

AMONG THE FIRST LEGENDS

Two of the earliest architects of jazz were Buddy Bolden and James Reese Europe. Charles "Buddy" Bolden (1868–1941) from New Orleans was part of a "shouting congregation" church. He mastered the cornet before the age of eight. He is said to have created the first jazz band in the early twentieth century, although the term *jazz* was rarely used until the 1930s.[14] The band combined several of the available musical sounds, including ragtime, gospel music, and especially the blues. Testimonies abound, though a good deal is unverifiable legend. Louis Armstrong called him "the blowingest man since Gabriel."[15] Although we have no recordings of Bolden, the evidence points to his playing ragtime, with a blues undertone.

The second figure, James Reese Europe (1880–1919), distinguished himself as a soldier. He created a jazz band called the Clef Club. The band played at Carnegie Hall in 1912, a benefit concert in support of the Colored Music Settlement School. Long before the great concerts of White bandleaders such as Paul Whiteman, George Gershwin, and Benny

---

humor, the musical talent, and the improvised variations on the tune so characteristic of great jazz.

[12]"Joe Pass – 'Ain't Misbehavin',"" YouTube video, 5:51, posted by "dave gould," July 23, 2014, www.youtube.com/watch?v=p_kUJa1PueM.

[13]Most musicians possess "fake books" such as *The Real Book*, which contains hundreds of song charts with melody and chords ("changes"), thus enabling almost anyone conversant with the genre to play any tune, with or without other musicians.

[14]See Donald M. Marquis, *In Search of Buddy Bolden: First Man of Jazz* (Baton Rouge: Louisiana State University Press, 2005).

[15]Cited in Marshall W. Stearns, *The Story of Jazz* (New York: Oxford University Press, 1956), 70.

Goodman in the famed Hall, this event was truly a landmark. What likely boosted Jim Europe's renown was his travel to France with his military band early in World War I. There, French soldiers would bring their compositions to him, and he would transform them into improvised music. Many of the songs were about tragedy on the battlefield. So, the sounds of the blues, which the band played, resonated with the audiences. Above all Jim Europe was adamant about the authenticity of Black music. Along the lines we have already examined, he said, "We colored people have our own music that is part of us. It's the product of our souls; it's been created by the sufferings and miseries of our race."[16]

Jazz has had its share of White participants, as we have mentioned. Surely, real jazz can be played by any musician, regardless of his or her background or skin color. Yet it is still curious that the first recording of a group calling itself a jazz band was made up of White musicians. The Original Dixieland Jazz Band recorded "Livery Stable Blues" in 1917. It featured gags, such as a clarinet sounding like a rooster, a cornet producing a whinnying sound, and the trombone sounding like a cow. In terms of musical technique, it was sloppy, but it became a huge bestseller.[17] Much, if not all, of the music was borrowed (to use a generous word) from Black music, including the vaudeville shows of yore. A lawsuit based on plagiarism against Nick Larocca, the band leader, was dismissed because the music was considered in poor taste. Most jazz lovers would not call this music authentic jazz, but it had the effect of introducing the music to a White audience.

LOUIS ARMSTRONG

What we might call the first authentic jazz recordings must be credited to Joseph "King" Oliver, Louis Armstrong, Ferdinand "Jelly Roll" Morton, and their colleagues. Their work helps us understand jazz aesthetics, and we are fortunate to possess numerous recordings of these artists.

---

[16]Maurice Peress, *Dvořák to Duke Ellington* (New York: Oxford University Press, 2004), 65.
[17]"Original Dixieland Jass Band – Livery Stable Blues (1917)," YouTube video, 3:10, posted by "peppopb," November 2, 2007, www.youtube.com/watch?v=5WojNaU4-kI.

Their work has been interpreted in a singular way by the Dutch art historian and jazz connoisseur, H. R. Rookmaaker (1922–1977). He holds an important place in the appreciation of jazz by a European, and he helpfully makes an explicit connection of jazz to the Christian faith.[18] Rookmaaker loved the great pioneer "King" Oliver (1881–1938), who became a leading light in the jazz world. He mentored many musicians, but the best known among them is Louis Armstrong (1901–1971). What made Oliver's music so compelling? From the recordings and a few verbal accounts, we know that he played with authority and with clean, assured articulation. A part of the New Orleans diaspora to Chicago, he hired many New Orleans musicians. The cornet in such a group was clearly the melodic leader. Recording technology had not yet kept up with the amazing spirit of ensemble playing that characterized these bands. On their first soundtrack sessions, he and Louis Armstrong had to be moved to twenty feet away from the microphone! By all accounts, Oliver's style was filled with the blues. At the same time, his band was always in demand for dances. It must not be forgotten that early on, jazz was dance music.[19]

H. R. Rookmaaker did a great deal of good by editing jazz records (mostly for the Fontana label, a subsidiary of the Dutch Philips Records) and writing numerous articles, as well as the groundbreaking book, *Jazz, Blues and Spirituals*. These contain many judgments, some controversial, about jazz aesthetics. In his view, King Oliver was an ensemble man and reluctant to feature too many solos. Rookmaaker even claims he did not improvise, nor did the members of his band. He

---

[18]H. R. Rookmaaker was one of the first Europeans to collect and write about American jazz. He was a leader in Francis Schaeffer's L'Abri movement. See his *Jazz, Blues, Spirituals* (Phillipsburg, NJ: P&R, 2020). For a recent engagement with Rookmaaker's legacy, see Jonathan A. Anderson and William A. Dyrness, *Modern Art and the Life of a Culture: The Religious Impulses of Modernism* (Downers Grove, IL: IVP Academic, 2016).

[19]Check out his immortal Creole Jazz Band recordings (Richmond, IN: 1923): "The Best of King Oliver's Creole Jazz Band (1923 recordings) | Jazz Music," YouTube video, 1:15:55, posted by "HALIDONMUSIC," February 17, 2016, www.youtube.com/watch?v=TE6HRi2E-dc. The best shorter account of his life and music remains Frederic Ramsey Jr., "King Oliver and His Creole Jazz Band," in *Jazzmen*, ed. Frederic Ramsey Jr. and Charles Edward Smith (New York: Harcourt, Brace, 1939), 59-91.

compares New Orleans bands from the early 1920s to baroque music, with its "pure polyphony" and argues that Oliver's music is deeply joyful, in the spirit of Bach. He contends that both were inspired by Christian principles: "We believe [this remarkable state of affairs] can only be explained by a common spiritual background. Bach's context was a very positively Bible-believing Christianity."[20] Rookmaaker went on to say that when Louis Armstrong parted company with Oliver, he proceeded to develop a much more individualistic style, submitting to the spirit of the age.

Figure 9.2. Louis "Pops" Armstrong, the ambassador of traditional jazz

---

[20]Rookmaaker, *Jazz, Blues and Spirituals*, 215. While Rookmaaker may have been something of a purist, his frustration with the middle class was shared by his colleague and close friend Francis A. Schaeffer. The quest for authenticity ("reality," as they liked to call it) was fundamental to their L'Abri message. Many in my own generation shared this quest and responded in various ways, not all of them healthy. But it is true that the love of jazz in the twentieth century was often a response to the emptiness perceived in the surrounding culture.

I believe that this finding is hasty. There are a number of solo moments in Oliver's recordings, and although he would certainly exercise greater freedom, Armstrong's solos never departed significantly from the ensemble. A solo need not mean individualism of an unhealthy kind. We are fortunate to be able to experience much of Armstrong's entire œuvre, and I am reluctant to identify a sort of "fall" with his development. True, there is more solo work in some of Armstrong's earliest recordings when he was on his own. There is something truly magical about them, and many believe that his "Hot Five" and "Hot Seven" recordings on the Okeh label in Chicago (1925; 1927) are among the great treasures of New Orleans jazz, a marvel to behold.[21] Armstrong never stood still. He not only played powerfully down through the decades but reflected on jazz and life during his times. He is rightly nicknamed "Pops" and is nearly universally revered by musicians and the public.

And yet Rookmaaker was onto something important. When asked what drew him and many others to jazz, the White, Dutch scholar, gave two answers. First, the entertainment music of the time was "so empty, so superficial, that a good shot of something was necessary."[22] For him, jazz was a fresh response in the face of such vacuous music. But second, jazz also gave westerners the opportunity to protest the middle class bourgeois lifestyle.[23] In fact, the two observations, freshness and the anti-bourgeois polemic, are related if not identical. To what kind of contemporary entertainment music was he referring? He does not say, exactly. A good deal of remarkable modern music was being created in the early twentieth century. It was the era of Stravinsky, Prokofiev, Ravel, Schönberg, and many others. These were hardly empty and superficial. My guess is that Rookmaaker was referring to the likes of Tin Pan Alley, White swing bands, low-level ragtime, and even some of the rhythm and blues music, which must have come across as lacking in depth. He was not alone in drawing attention to the critique of social

---

[21]See "Louis Armstrong and his Hot Five Complete Volume 1," YouTube video, 36:16, posted by "Peter Menard," December 18, 2016, www.youtube.com/watch?v=BfORYuSJXTY.

[22]H. R. R. Rookmaaker, "Rock, The Background to Modern Music: An Interview," in *The Complete Works of Hans Rookmaaker*, ed. Marleen Hengelaar-Rookmaaker (Carlisle, UK: Piquant, 2002), 2:377.

[23]Rookmaaker, "Rock," 377.

injustice at the center of blues and jazz. For example, regarding a blues song by Big Bill Broonzy, he states, "It is a song which shows that in spite of their circumstances, the blacks did not display rampant revolutionary sentiments. It also shows that they had not yet learned to express the concept of human rights."[24] I think this is a questionable assessment. Indeed, today scholars are increasingly recognizing the role of jazz in addressing social issues.[25]

In addition, there is truth to the idea that Oliver's music carries a certain joy, a certain peaceful confidence, throughout its bluesy sounds. It is also true that solo playing gradually became a more defining characteristic of jazz and has remained so ever since. Ted Gioia agrees that earlier there was a unique sense of the *whole* in early jazz. He even asserts that one of the challenges of the New Orleans sound for modern ears is precisely the fixed roles each instrument played. This can be a stumbling block to modern ears: "[We have] . . . the very unmodern aesthetic vision underpinning early New Orleans jazz music. Unlike later jazz, with its more 'democratic' reliance on individual solos, the New Orleans pioneers created a music in which the *group* was primary, in which each instrument was expected to play a specific role, not assert its independence."[26]

Thus, without a doubt, ensemble playing characterized early jazz. Yet there was never quite the contradiction with taking solos that Rookmaaker diagnosed. The best soloists were always conscious of the larger ensemble. What made jazz unique, among other things, was its creative way to redefine playing the instruments. Tone production, as well as ensemble playing, was paramount. Sidney Bechet, the great clarinetist and soprano sax player, is said to have told a student to vary the single note: "See how many ways you can play the note—growl it, smear it, flat it, sharp it, do anything you want to it. . . . It's like talking."[27] Thus, while it took a while to develop a fully individual sense of playing, the best individualism was never isolated from the group.

---

[24]Rookmaaker, *Jazz, Blues and Spirituals*, 190.
[25]See John Paul Lederach and Angela Jill Lederach, *When Blood and Bones Cry Out: Journeys Through the Soundscape of Healing and Reconciliation* (New York: Oxford University Press, 2010).
[26]Gioia, *History of Jazz*, 48-53.
[27]Quoted in David Axe, *Jazz Cultures* (Berkeley: University of California Press, 2002), 27.

Importantly, and never far beneath the surface, was the context of racism in which early jazz developed. We have already noted the ways that it profoundly influenced the growth of earlier musical genres. And it would be easy to ignore the concern for race issues underneath the amazing music created by these early jazz masters. As I have already mentioned, Armstrong seemed to have fooled many folks because of his bubbly onstage personality. Offstage was another story. He famously accused President Eisenhower of being "two-faced" and having no guts during the Little Rock, Arkansas, integration crisis in 1957. Following the Supreme Court decision in *Brown v. Board of Education* in 1954, nine Black children were denied entry into Central High School. When President Eisenhower refused to enforce their right to enroll, Armstrong remarked: "It's getting so bad a colored man hasn't got any country."[28] He sang an unprintable parody of the national anthem to a reporter, and he refused to go on a goodwill tour behind the Iron Curtain. Eisenhower did change his mind, and Armstrong backed off somewhat.[29] His anti-racism made its way into the music. In one of his best-known songs, "Black and Blue," he crooned, "My only sin is in my skin; What did I do to be so black and blue?"[30] Armstrong is a fitting musician to highlight our theme of misery to joy, particularly because his onstage persona is so cheerful. We are learning through his extensive diaries just how sensitive he was to racial injustice and human suffering. Armstrong was not a civil rights warrior. But neither was he the Uncle Tom figure some of his colleagues accused him of being.[31]

---

[28]People were taken aback by Armstrong's outspokenness. He was known to stay away from politics, but this time he spoke out: "The way they are treating my people in the South, the government can go to hell." See David Margolick, "The Day Louis Armstrong Made Noise," *New York Times*, September 23, 2007, www.nytimes.com/2007/09/23/opinion/23margolick.html.

[29]This incident is chronicled in many places. The most level-headed is Terry Teachout, *Pops*, 334-36 .

[30]One of the most moving recordings is the original from 1929: "BLACK AND BLUE by Louis Armstrong 1929 BLUES!!," YouTube video, 3:05, posted by "cdbpdx," December 4, 2009, www.youtube.com/watch?v=gHLTI2cMCQk.

[31]See Ricky Riccardi, *Heart Full of Rhythm: The Big Band Years of Louis Armstrong* (New York: Oxford University Press, 2021), 195-206.

JELLY ROLL MORTON

Two more pioneers should be added in order to supplement our account of the aesthetics of jazz at its foundation. The first is the pianist and composer "Jelly Roll" Morton (1890–1941). His real name was Ferdinand Joseph La Mothe, from a line of New Orleans Creoles. Morton could stretch the truth in order to accommodate his boastful claims. For example, he declared that he had invented jazz, earning him considerable scorn. He began playing music in brothels, known as "sporting houses" and was nearly disowned by his churchgoing great-grandmother, who had brought him up. He often denied his African roots and claimed European, Creole ascendency.

We are fortunate to possess a series of recordings of his thoughts, over eight hours of them, hosted by Alan Lomax for the Library of Congress. Illustrating at the piano, Morton takes us through the vicissitudes of jazz and gives us the first serious analysis of the aesthetics of jazz music.[32]

Figure 9.3. "Jelly Roll" Morton (third from the left), a pianist and composer, once said, "Rejoice at the death and cry at the birth: New Orleans sticks close to the Scriptures."

[32]See Alan Lomax, interviews of Jelly Roll Morton, American Folk Song Collection, Library of Congress, 8 hours, 59 minutes.

Many argue that because jazz was "born" in brothels in Storyville, the famous New Orleans red-light district, there has always been an association between jazz and a degree of immorality. There is perhaps some truth to this. Many of the early jazzmen (almost all were men), including Morton, took jobs in these barrelhouses and were practiced in the concomitant social skills. Yet the picture is more nuanced. Few of the musicians played in these places by choice.[33] And other influences, such as marching bands, were as significant as the more vaudeville styles developed in the bordellos. The often-made gratuitous association of jazz with brothels is at best a caricature, and at worst a great slight on the genius of the genre. Besides, jazz soon moved out of these places altogether and began to be understood as art music.[34]

Morton soon left Storyville and wandered around the country. The high point of his career was arguably his stay in Chicago from 1923 to 1935. Not only did he prove himself able as a promoter, but he composed and played a number of masterpieces that have come down over the decades. He also founded the Red Hot Peppers, with its matchless orchestral artistry.[35] Gioia comments that Morton was unchallenged in his genius until Duke Ellington pushed the limits of creativity even further in the following decade: "But above all, in his mastery of ensemble interaction—so essential to the New Orleans aesthetic—this band remains the paragon example to this day."[36]

DUKE ELLINGTON

The best example of the possibility of blending individuals into a group, while yet keeping them distinctive, has to be Edward Kennedy "Duke" Ellington and his band. I believe he was America's greatest composer. His output was enormous. Ellington (1899–1974) composed hundreds of songs and several suites. Again, the bluesy marching band sounds

---

[33]Stearns, *Story of Jazz*, 72.
[34]See James McCalla, *Jazz: A Listener's Guide* (Englewood Cliffs, NJ: Prentice-Hall, 1982), 63.
[35]"Jelly Roll Morton - Red Hot Pepper," YouTube video, 3:15, posted by "OnlyJazzHQ," January 21, 2013, www.youtube.com/watch?v=etiqFMKeK60.
[36]Gioia, *History of Jazz*, 41.

combined with extraordinary improvisation. It has been said that his orchestrations were like paintings, with varied colors and dynamics, all
serving the whole.[37] After all, he started out as a visual artist![38]

Duke had the extraordinary ability to attract first-rate musicians to his
band. Each one was not only first-rate, but also had distinctive traits.
Trumpeter Bubber Miley could produce special resonances out of the
instrument, such as his signature plunger-mute sound, that might have
been considered gags, except that they fit perfectly into the ensemble.
Likewise, Miley's replacement, Cootie Williams, brought a unique style,
and perhaps a greater depth, to the trumpet that then added a special
character to the Ellington band's distinctive sound. With a melodic style
inspired by his Baptist church, he shone on pieces such as *The Shepherd
Watches His Flock by Night*, dedicated to the marvelous pastor to jazz
musicians, John Gensel. "Tricky" Joe Nanton could make the trombone
growl and stay musical along with it, and Johnny Hodges was the epitome
of a lofty, blues-like, ballad player who was described as "honey." Somehow,
these splendid individuals blended to form the beautiful symphonic
sounds of a jazz orchestra.

Like so many others, Ellington was very sensitive to race issues. He
declared that one of his life's purposes was to educate people in race
matters. He was often misread as an Uncle Tom figure—the same accusation Gillespie lodged against Louis Armstrong (which was unfair in my
view, certainly to Armstrong and Ellington). This is in part because Duke
claimed not to be interested in politics, and in part because he was such
a worldly figure that some thought he could not be bothered. A number
of times the Black press accused him of complicity with racist practices.
When he played at the Cotton Club, he had to accept the management's

---

[37]See Andrea Davis Pinkney and Brian Pinkney, "Rejoice the Legacy," online exhibit from
2014 Arbuthnot Honor Lecture, University of Minnesota, http://gallery.lib.umn.edu
/exhibits/show/pinkney/preforming-arts/ellington.

[38]One of the best biographies of Duke Ellington is by Edward John Hasse, *Beyond Category:
The Life and Genius of Duke Ellington* (Boston: Da Capo, 1995). See also Terry Teachout,
Duke: A Life of Duke Ellington (Garden City, NY: Avery, 2013); Stanley Dance, *The World
of Duke Ellington* (New York: Scribner, 1970); Stuart Nicholson, *Reminiscing in Tempo: A
Portrait of Duke Ellington* (Boston: Northeastern University Press, 1999).

terms: Whites only in the audience, light-colored Black performers on stage. But he was still profoundly concerned with racial justice. He sometimes had to hide his views in order to get them published. A thoughtful article in the *New Yorker* captures the spirit: "His most extraordinary talent, however, may have been for making the best of tainted opportunities. For the big revues, with their plots about Black savages and threatened maidens, he devised music of sophistication and cheekily exotic allure, under such titles as 'Jungle Blues,' 'Jungle Night in Harlem' and—a sinister little masterpiece—'The Mooche.'"[39] Ellington's own comments reveal his sensitivity to and awareness of the larger picture: "'What we could not say openly, we expressed in music,' Ellington wrote in the British magazine *Rhythm*, in 1931, trying to explain the Negro musical tradition that had grown up in America, music 'forged from the very white heat of our sorrows.'"[40]

Throughout his career, Duke wrote music that showcased the Black experience. The titles alone tell the tale: "Black Beauty," "Harlem Speaks," "Creole Rhapsody," "Symphony in Black," and above all, the marvelous lyrical suite *Black, Brown and Beige*.[41] Ellington described the last of these as "a parallel to the history of the Negro." It is a suite in three movements, each representing one aspect of the struggle of Black people through slavery, Jim Crow, and acceptance in the twentieth century. "Black"

---

[39]"Duke Ellington - The Mooche - Best version," YouTube video, 6:39, posted by "Marcia Luciano Vieira," October 31, 2011, www.youtube.com/watch?v=SFqdebJy290. See also Duke and Louis Armstrong in a rare recording: "The Mooche - Louis Armstrong & Duke Ellington," YouTube video, 3:35, posted by "Klar Name," January 4, 2010, www.youtube .com/watch?v=20GsgjlEFWg. See also Michelle R. Scott and Earle Brooks, "Duke Ellington's Melodies Carried his Message of Social Justice," *The Conversation*, https:// theconversation.com/duke-ellingtons-melodies-carried-his-message-of-social-justice -115602. 77n278. See his *Music Is My Mistress* (Garden City, NY: Doubleday, 1973), 471; Teachout, *Duke*, 226-34; Hasse, *Beyond Category*, 261-63.

[40]Claudia Roth Pierpont, "Black, Brown, and Beige, Duke Ellington's Music and Race in America," *New Yorker*, May 10, 2010, www.newyorker.com/magazine/2010/05/17/black -brown-and-beige/.

[41]Several recordings exist, including the reconstituted original. The one with vocalist Mahalia Jackson (1958) is a true classic: "Duke Ellington, Mahalia Jackson - Black, Brown and Beige, Pt. 1," YouTube video, 8:14, posted by "Jazz Everyday!," March 11, 2016, www.youtube .com/watch?v=o06HwF2PfXw.

Figure 9.4. Duke Ellington didn't care for the term *jazz*, but he became one of its most celebrated composers.

reflected on the cruelties of forced labor. "Brown" carried references to emancipation and the participation of Black people in American wars. "Beige" was a reference to the lighter colored people of Harlem. The piece received mixed reviews. On the positive side, Duke was called "a black Stravinsky." On the negative side, it was considered incoherent and lacking drive. Harvey G. Cohen, in his excellent study *Duke Ellington's America*, defends Duke in a number of ways.[42] He suggests that negative reviews at the time may have come from the perception that he had held back (which he had) from saying all that he had to say in *Black, Brown and Beige* which may have been felt by the audience, which, incidentally, included Eleanor Roosevelt, Leopold Stokowski, Count Basie, and Frank Sinatra.

In addition to the many strands and traditions of Black music, he managed to incorporate certain elements of European orchestration and timbre. His music could be pensive and rich, and it was always full of swing. He did not think he had to choose between being an entertainer

---

[42]Harvey G. Cohen, *Duke Ellington's America* (Chicago: University of Chicago Press, 2010).

and a contemporary classical composer. He generously collaborated with contemporary greats, such as Louis Armstrong, Count Basie, and John Coltrane. One of his many masterpieces, "It Don't Mean a Thing If It Ain't Got That Swing," was recorded hundreds of times. He recorded an uplifting version performed with his lifelong friend Ella Fitzgerald, who moves into "scat" singing, a convention in Afro-American improvisation using "nonsense" words in rhythm.[43]

In the last decades of his life, he focused on sacred music, composing three sacred oratorios in a jazz-like idiom. He considered these compositions to be his most significant. He was indeed beyond category, as we might say, *sui generis*. Throughout his life and work, he espoused the view that racism should be attacked by subversion through good music, rather than frontally by aggressive activism. What he could not say openly in words, he expressed in his music.[44]

ALL THAT JAZZ

During the early formation of jazz, crucial aesthetic principles were in evidence. Jazz was born out of a grand synthesis of its many precursors, including spirituals, field hollers, blues, ragtime, popular song, and marching bands. It exhibited a swinging rhythm, improvisation, a blues feeling, and awareness of social issues and protest against racism, whether implicit or explicit. While the earliest jazz was an ensemble affair, soloing and individualism gradually emerged, though never at the expense of the group.

And what about the relationship between jazz and faith? Oliver, Armstrong, Morton, Duke. The Christian faith of these early pioneers was not evangelical, at least in the sense of the modern definition.[45] Nevertheless,

---

[43]"Ella Fitzgerald & Duke Ellington – 'It Don't Mean a Thing (If It Ain't Got That Swing)," YouTube video, 7:14, posted by "SpatialBlues," October 25, 2015, www.youtube.com /watch?v=1gtYvN_mH64.

[44]See Michelle R. Scott and Earl Brooks, "Duke Ellington's Melodies Carried His Message of Social Justice," *The Conversation*, April 24, 2019, https://theconversation.com/duke -ellingtons-melodies-carried-his-message-of-social-justice-115602/.

[45]See, for example, David Bebbington's quadrilateral of "conversionism, activism, biblicism and crucicentrism," as described in Mark A. Noll, *The Rise of Evangelicalism: The Age of Edwards, Whitefield, and the Wesleys* (Downers Grove, IL: InterVarsity Press, 2003), 19.

as far as we can tell, they all had a deep sense of the reality of God, and of his presence through suffering.

King Oliver exhibited his faith in some poignant letters to his sister when he was destitute and close to death. He wrote his sister, "Dear Sister, I'm still out of work. Since the road house closed I haven't hit a note. But I've got a lot to thank God for. Because I eat and sleep. . . . Look like every time one door closes the Good Lord opens another."[46] Two months before his death (April 10, 1938) he wrote these moving lines: "Don't think I'm afraid because I wrote what I did [about the challenges of living in New York], I am trying to live near to the Lord than ever before. So I feel like the Good Lord will take care of me."[47] This is more than a sociological faith. It is deep and real. Rookmaaker connects Oliver's faith to his music, and he sees both as exhibiting confidence and generosity in the midst of adversity.[48]

With Louis Armstrong matters are less clear. He was baptized Roman Catholic and grew up in a Protestant culture. He also enjoyed very close relations with a Lithuanian Jewish family, the Karnofkys, who treated him like a son. His manager Joe Glaser gave him a star of David, which he wore the rest of his life. In his last recollections he comments that the Jews have suffered even more than Black people from "ungodly treatment."[49] Armstrong did read his Bible often, and he occasionally performed spirituals. *Louis Armstrong and the Good Book* (1958) contains many standards, such as "Go Down Moses" and "Swing Low, Sweet Chariot." He also recorded an enigmatic song called "Faith" from the musical *I Had a Ball* (1964). The lyrics include these lines:

Well now faith can give you wings to fly

True faith can make you fly so high

Yes faith can touch the sky

---

[46]Frederick Ramsey Jr. and Charles Edward Smith, *Jazzmen* (New York: Harcourt, Brace, 1939), 89.

[47]Ramsey and Smith, *Jazzmen*, 91.

[48]Rookmaaker, *Jazz, Blues, Spirituals*, 215.

[49]Louis Armstrong, "Louis Armstrong + the Jewish Family in New Orleans, La, the Year of 1907" (Louis Armstrong House and Archives at Queens College/CUNY). See Dalton Anthony Jones, "Louis Armstrong's 'Karnofsky Document': The Reaffirmation of Social Death and the Afterlife of Emotional Labor," *Music & Politics* 9, no. 1 (2015).

You can solve the riddle of it

If you got a little of it.

Sometimes, it is hard to tell in his music what is entertainment, what is sincere, and what is tongue-in-cheek. But from an overview of Armstrong's life and thoughts, what is certain is how aware he was of the suffering of his people.

Jelly Roll Morton was a "very devout Catholic" according to his companion Anita Gonzales. In a fascinating article written in 1921 for the *Ladies' Home Journal*, the author boldly states, "Many of those considered founding fathers of jazz music from New Orleans, King Oliver, Jelly Roll Morton, and Louis Armstrong were all brought up in church and church music played a very important role in their musical development. The Negro spirituals also played a most important role in the birth of the music we today call 'jazz.'"[50] Indeed, it was Morton who famously said, "Rejoice at the death and cry at the birth: New Orleans sticks close to the Scriptures."[51] These are extraordinary words from a musician who has claimed to invent jazz and who is one of its most prolific architects.

And finally, Duke Ellington. He proclaimed his faith often and publicly. His music exhibits the narrative of misery to joy as powerfully as anyone, as revealed in his masterpiece, "Come Sunday":

Lord, dear Lord I've loved, God almighty

God of love, please look down and see my people through

Lord, dear Lord I've loved, God almighty

God of love, please look down and see my people through

I believe that sun and moon up in the sky

When the day is gray

---

[50]Anne Shaw Faulkner, "Does Jazz Put the Sin in Syncopation?," Ladies Home Journal (August 1921): 16-34, http://arcadiasystems.org/academia/syncopate.html.

[51]See Marshall Bowden, "Spiritual Jazz: From New Orleans to Coltrane and Beyond," *New Directions in Music*, www.newdirectionsinmusic.com/spiritual-jazz-from-new-orleans-to-coltrane-and-beyond/.

I know it, clouds passing by

He'll give peace and comfort

To every troubled mind

Come Sunday, oh come Sunday

That's the day

Often we feel weary

But he knows our every care

Go to him in secret

He will hear your every prayer

Lillies on the valley

They neither toll nor spin

And flowers bloom in spring time

Birds sing

Often we feel weary

But he knows our every care

Go to him in secret

He will hear your every prayer

Up from dawn till sunset

Man work hard all the day

Come Sunday, oh come Sunday

That's the day.

Jazz has never stood still. Its history embodies the improvisation that characterizes the music. But what provides continuity across the stages of its development is the narrative that moves from deep misery to inextinguishable joy.

10

JAZZ AT MIDLIFE

BEBOP AND COOL

In their fascination with technical virtuosity and harmonic complexity, fueled by an engaging combination of restless curiosity and guileless ambition, [the bebop musicians] were self-consciously progressive.

SCOTT DEVEAUX

As jazz reached its third decade, it had something like a midlife transition. I can well remember my mother telling me that when Benny Goodman came around to the beach club where she grew up, it was a gala evening with well-dressed men and women ready to do acrobatic dances such as the Lindy Hop. In my teen years, I can remember when the Lester Lanin Band came to our own youthful events. But these bands didn't last as jazz entered a new phase. Although there were certainly ongoing performances in the older swing style, newer forms emerged, especially bebop and cool.

Our primary concern is with the aesthetics of jazz and the movement from deep sorrow to inextinguishable joy informed by a biblical faith, but it is helpful to bear in mind the critical milestones in the evolution of jazz. Gary Giddens and Scott DeVeaux divide jazz history into four phases.[1] These are roughly chronological, though they are not simply succeeding stylistic schools. Rather, they are stages that take their place within the overall cultural world in which they are situated.

(1) The first phase (1890s–1920s) they call "the period of genesis."[2] Here we are reminded that jazz had its origins in the Black South, and particularly in the city of New Orleans. The authors tell us this is "where a mixture of musical and cultural influences combined to create a freewheeling, largely improvised, blues-based music that suited every social gathering, entertaining the living and commemorating the dead." I would add a word of caution here. The expressions "freewheeling" and "largely improvised" might give the impression of a total spontaneity, whereas, as we have seen, the music was anything but purely extemporaneous.

(2) The second phase (1920s–1950s) saw the transformation of jazz "from a community-based phenomenon to an authentic art of unlimited potential."[3] In this phase jazz became international. Its influence could be felt in music outside of its immediate purview. And, unsurprisingly, opinions varied widely. Europeans had mixed views. Perhaps understandably, the French reaction was varied. On the one hand it was believed that this music represented the worst of American imperialism, with its mechanized rhythms and consumerism.[4] On the other hand, there were wildly enthusiastic responses, such as those of Rookmaaker. Even among the French, the *Hot Club de France* organization, spearheaded by Hugues Panassié, was among the first to recognize the great freshness and virtues of early jazz.[5]

(3) Giddens and DeVeaux argue that the third phase (1950s–1970s) was defined by "the limits of modernism," which meant both greater artistic freedom but also the alienation of the general public. Two apparently contradictory genres emerged in this period. First, the rather elitist bebop,

---

[1] Gary Giddens and Scott DeVeaux, *Jazz* (New York: W. W. Norton, 2009), 605-6.
[2] Giddens and DeVeaux, *Jazz*, 605.
[3] Giddens and DeVeaux, *Jazz*, 605.
[4] This was the view of many French people right after World War I. See, for example, Robert Aron and André Dandieu, *Le Cancer Américain* (Paris: Rieder, 1931; repr., Geneva: L'Âge d'Homme, 2008).
[5] Hugues Panassié, *Hot Jazz: The Guide to Swing Music* (New York: M. Witmark & Sons, 1936).

which we will discuss in this chapter. Bebop was more for listeners than for dancing. Jazz became more academic. Second, with no discernable relation, this is the period in which more accessible genres such as rhythm and blues and rock 'n' roll came into prominence.

(4) The fourth and final phase (1970–present day), is more classical for two reasons. First, it became more tribal. That is, it was confined to the academy and to festivals supported by grants. It has become international but has lost popularity in North America. Second, they argue that musicians today are defined by the past, to the point, negatively, of limiting their creativity, or positively, of opening new avenues, such as fusions and "daring explorations."[6] Simply put, fusion is a combination of styles that were originally separate. It often involves using instruments and rhythms from two different genres, such as jazz rock. The earliest forms include Afro-Cuban and other Latin sounds, such as the habanera. Popular fusions include Brazilian jazz fusion, which uses rhythms such as the bossa nova and the samba combined with modern jazz arrangements. One thinks of the television series *Jazz* by Ken Burns and the role of specialists such as Winton Marsalis in the promotion of jazz at Lincoln Center.[7] One thinks as well of the profusion of talented younger musicians coming out of places such as Juilliard or Rutgers, who are quite creative and often fresh in their approach.

MIDLIFE WITHOUT THE CRISIS

These phases do not stand in absolute contrast one to the other. Still, there is considerable divergence between the era of swing music and modernism, or "bebop" as the new style would soon be called. Swing bands could be White or Black, but they had in common the big orchestra, a driving rhythm, and an invitation to dance. Inevitably, though, these larger entertainment ensembles would decline. Some of the reasons were

---

[6]It might be confusing to label this entire period as "classical" simply because the word connotes a sort of conservatism that is only characteristic of some of the styles. Alongside that there are all kinds of experimentation.

[7]Ken Burns, *Jazz* (PBS Home Video, 2005), DVD.

simply practical. It was exhausting for the musicians to live on the road, be it on trains or buses. Though very popular to audiences, the cost of running a band was increasingly expensive. And thus there was, even in the most remarkable orchestras, a kind of fatigue. Count Basie and Duke Ellington were becoming senior statesmen rather than cutting-edge artists. More especially, though, it was the conditions surrounding World War II that contributed most to the demise of the big band.

The war was devastating for Europeans. For Americans, it was a mixed occasion. Though many lives were lost, the *Pax Americana* was ushered in with its confidence and optimism. But soon thereafter, doubts began to emerge. Newer vogues began to displace the big band culture. Younger Americans began to tire of the sweeter sounds of the swing orchestras. Though Glenn Miller's "In the Mood" and "Moonlight Serenade" could bring tears to the eyes of an older generation, there was something empty about the music to young people. It is often thought that the 1960s were the truly revolutionary times that ushered in the youthful rebellion of "drugs, sex, and rock 'n' roll." But historian George Marsden argues that it was in fact the 1950s that portended for the contemporary era even more significantly.[8] Marsden contends that although the White, Protestant churchgoing majority defined American values on the surface, underneath was an instability, a restlessness where "the center could not hold."[9] This is in great part because the self-assured pragmatic liberalism in the doctrine of the majority did not listen to minority voices, to women, and especially Black folks. Despite some progress, this is still sadly the case.

Yet, those voices appeared. If the swing era defined the pragmatic liberalism of the dominant culture, the emerging voices of styles such as bebop and rhythm and blues was the alternative. In exchange for Doris Day's "How Much Is That Doggy in the Window?" came Louis

---

[8]George Marsden, *The Twilight of the American Enlightenment: The 1950s and the Crisis of American Liberalism* (New York: Basic Books, 2014).

[9]The expression "the center could not hold" is from William Butler Yeats's celebrated poem, "The Second Coming," a post–World War I commentary: *William Butler Yeats: The Collected Poems* (Stanstead, UK: Wordsworth, 1994), 158.

Jordan's "Saturday Night Fish Fry" and his "Caldonia."[10] Though mild by later standards, the Jordan songs are decidedly African American, bluesy, and urban. And then, of course, came its direct descendant: rock 'n' roll.[11]

Perhaps one of the fascinating issues about bebop is how it is embedded in the entire history of jazz. Jazz musicians have always been entertainers. Yet at the same time they have been creative innovators. As Ted Gioia writes, "For the jazz musician soon proved to be a restless soul, at one moment fostering the tradition, at another shattering it, mindless of the pieces."[12] Bebop was certainly jazz music. Despite the purists' rejection of it, the music was firmly within the tradition. Yet it was developed more or less underground, not in the dance halls but in late-night jam sessions. Small groups were favored over large bands. Solos were charged, sometimes incredibly, with steady streams of eighth and sixteenth notes, using offbeat phrasing.

CONTROVERSY

The new styles were controversial. Conservatives found them too radical. Others embraced them as the only real hope for African American tradition. Aesthetically, there was both continuity and discontinuity with the older music. The blues element was certainly present but in a decidedly modern guise. Harmonies were more complex and improvisation more intense.

Though one can find roots in the older music, the newer sounds arrived with "terrifying suddenness" to some.[13] This naturally aroused

---

[10]Compare "Doris Day-How much is that doggie," YouTube video, 2:24, posted by "valdur raak," July 10, 2007, www.youtube.com/watch?v=BR7yRLF5ENk to "Louis Jordan - Saturday Night Fish Fry," YouTube video, 5:05, posted by "mrspats1," June 23, 2009, www .youtube.com/watch?v=b1QfXQakX2w or "Caldonia / Louis Jordan," YouTube video, 2:53, posted by "Elwood Yodogawa," August 28, 2008, www.youtube.com/watch?v =PR6pHtiNT_k.

[11]For further reading on the complex relation between rock music and the urban blues, see *Understanding Rock*, ed. John Covach and Graeme M. Boone (New York: Oxford University Press, 1997).

[12]Ted Gioia, *The History of Jazz* (New York: Oxford University Press, 1997), 200.

[13]Marshall W. Stearns, *The Story of Jazz* (New York: Oxford University Press, 1956), 219.

suspicion. Louis Armstrong broke with his usual diplomacy vis-à-vis other musicians and named bebop a "modern menace" and "no good."[14] French jazz specialist Hugues Panassié made a second career out of denouncing bebop. He argued in various ways that it was simply not jazz.[15]

On the other hand, there was a passionate push for the new music. Among non-musical factors was a greater assertiveness of Black people. Earlier they had either been hired by White leaders, such as Benny Goodman, or formed their own bands, such as the Chick Webb Band. But in both cases Black musicians were underpaid. Understandably, they grew weary of this discrimination. A more aggressive African American assertiveness characterized this new music. Some joined Islam, as much with religious conviction as for defense against the dominant culture. Musicians began to proclaim the new music *cool* rather than *hot*, and the epithet *cool* eventually made its way into mainstream culture.

Besides sociological reasons, there are some intangible reasons for this massive change. Musicians longed to get back to their musical roots, particularly the blues. Perhaps the most significant reason for the shift is captured by the word *ennui*. Charlie Parker at one point declared that he was "bored" with the stereotyped chords required in current popular music.[16] He engaged in a journey toward more freedom and self-expression. Along with many of the bebop artists, he concerned himself less with lyricism and more with rhythmic and harmonic complexity. If I am right, however couched, their quest was for something more transcendent, more exalted than what was being offered in much of the present-day music. Admittedly this was not necessarily a Christian aspiration, although it was not alien to it. As we will see, some musicians, such as John Coltrane, did embrace a resolutely God-centered experience.

---

[14]"Bop Will Kill Business unless It Kills Itself First," *Down Beat*, April 7, 1948, 2. Reprinted in *Keeping Time: Readings in Jazz History*, ed. Robert Walser (New York: Oxford University Press, 1999), 151–55.

[15]See his *The Real Jazz*, revised and enlarged ed. (Hartford, CT: A. S. Barnes, 1960), and his *La bataille du jazz* (Paris: Albin Michel, 1965).

[16]Stanley Crouch, *Kansas City Lightning: The Rise and Times of Charlie Parker* (New York: Harper, 2013), 34.

Most others were content to explore new avenues of musical expression and manifestations of freedom.

In my view, bebop stands in greater continuity with historic jazz than in a breach with it. True, its harmonic character was more sophisticated than in swing music. Bebop was often fast paced, with soloists using remarkable technique. The rhythm section was more intense and had more work for the bass player than in swing. Indeed, all the musicians in the ensemble shared equally in the improvisation. Possibly the blues character of bebop is harder to identify than in previous decades, though if one listens well, you will find it there.

A fair comparison of bebop to swing reveals far more connection to older jazz than first meets the ear. The thirty-two-bar structure (as well as the "twelve-bar blues") is there. The melody may be hidden under the improvisations, but it is there, at least tacitly. On top of that, we can find anticipations of bebop in earlier music: Art Tatum's advanced chords, Roy Eldridge's inventive trumpeting, Duke Ellington's modernistic orchestrations. And we find plenty of modern musicians who still played out of the American songbook and looked back at older phrasing: Erroll Garner's astonishing renditions of the jazz classics, using left-hand chords against the right-hand improvisations, Sarah Vaughan's often traditionalist recordings with Earl Hines and Nat King Cole, and Miles Davis's mastery of the blues.

GIANTS: GILLESPIE, PARKER, AND DAVIS

As with earlier jazz, bebop can best be understood through some of its chief proponents. In the interest of economy, I will examine just three of them, while recognizing that there are dozens more. These particular three figures could not be more different in disposition, yet they all played bebop. John Birks "Dizzy" Gillespie (1917–1993) earned his nickname because he loved to clown around. He capitalized on the image of the Black entertainer, but with tongue-in-cheek, keeping his White audiences fooled. His demeanor was unconventional: blowing his cheeks way out, bending his trumpet upward, and often sporting a beret (the look eventually defined the "beatnik" demeanor). But that was onstage. Offstage he had a different persona as a shrewd businessman, "keeping us all together," as Miles Davis put it.[17]

Dizzy played from a young age and was largely self-taught. At first, he sounded like his hero Roy Eldridge, but he soon developed his own signature style. He loved to hang out at Minton's Playhouse on 118th Street in Harlem. In many ways Minton's was the birthplace for bebop. While its jam sessions were technically against the union rules, these were never enforced. Imagine a platform composed of the greats: Thelonious Monk, Bud Powell, Kenny Clarke, Charlie Christian, Charlie Parker, and Dizzy Gillespie jamming together! Late-night hours, "cutting" contests, unrehearsed improvisations, how a jazz lover today would have treasured being a fly on the wall. Dizzy eventually moved from the fringes to being one of the United States' music ambassadors, a role that he filled uncomfortably.[18]

He excelled in rapid upward and downward scales and loved to quote bits of the classics such as the opening line of "Habañera" from Bizet's *Carmen*. His signature piece, "A Night in Tunisia," gives a good sense of his style.[19] Written in 1942, it was originally titled "Interlude," and while some unknown person renamed it "A Night in Tunisia," Dizzy had never been to North Africa. The opening bass line is Afro-Cuban, followed by an interlude, and then the piece goes into straight swing, affording Dizzy the opportunity to excel in rapid improvisation and a breathtaking use of scales.

Charlie "Bird" Parker (1920–1955) couldn't be more different from Dizzy. He is perhaps the most accomplished alto saxophonist of all time—and that is saying a great deal. Unfortunately, his personal life was filled with tragedy. Through drug abuse, he constantly interacted with unscrupulous underground figures. The great poet Ralph Ellison wrote that he

---

[17]Bobby Kosh, "What Miles Davis Can Teach Business About Innovation," *San Francisco Business Times*, March 9, 2017, www.bizjournals.com/sanfrancisco/news/2017/03/09/what -miles-davis-can-teach-businesses-about.html.

[18]See, Dizzy Gillespie, with Al Fraser, *To Be—Or Not to Bop* (Minneapolis: University of Minnesota Press, 2008); also, the excellent biography, Alyn Shipton, *Groovin' High: The Life of Dizzy Gillespie* (New York: Oxford University Press, 2001).

[19]"A Night In Tunisia," YouTube video, 5:34, posted by "Dizzy Gillespie – Topic," August 14, 2018, www.youtube.com/watch?v=eQHpwnXf0mI.

was "like a man dismembering himself with a dull razor on a spotlighted stage."[20] And, unlike the often-comic Gillespie, he was deadly serious in performance. Tapes show that he hardly moved when playing, though the sounds were surreal.[21]

Parker, more than anyone, combined jazz with high classical art. He was steeped in both. He was familiar with Hindemith, Stravinsky, Debussy, and even the electronic music composer Edgard Varèse. His roots were in Kansas City at the time of the Pendergast era. Parker knew the blues, and he either played them as individual pieces or integrated them into his music throughout. His heart-wrenching "Parker's Mood" is modern, but its roots are deeply in the suffering of his people.[22] It is a quintessential blues, but we might easily forget that it has lyrics:

> I'm feeling lowdown and blue, my heart's full of sorrow
>
> Don't hardly know what to do; where will I be tomorrow?
>
> Going to Kansas City. Want to go too?
>
> Though the friend cannot make it to Kansas City, the lyrics pursue,
>
> Don't hand your head when you see those six pretty horses pullin' me.
>
> Put a twenty dollar silver piece on my watch chain,
>
> Look at the smile on my face,
>
> And sing a little song to let the world know I'm really free.
>
> Don't cry for me, 'cause I'm going to Kansas City
>
> Come with me, if you want to go to Kansas City.

---

[20]Horace A. Porter, *Jazz Country: Ralph Ellision in America* (Iowa City: University of Iowa Press, 2001), 46.

[21]Listen to his masterpiece, "The Bird," at Carnegie Hall with an allstar quartet: "Charlie Parker-The Bird," YouTube video, 4:46, posted by "charlieparkerjazzart," February 11, 2012, www.youtube.com/watch?v=KYQCwoas3rk.

[22]"Parker's Mood - Charlie Parker," YouTube video, 3:09, posted by "Matt Lawton," October 25, 2012, www.youtube.com/watch?v=9Nn_Nghem60.

Here Kansas City, Parker's place of birth, becomes the metaphorical heaven. It's the movement from misery to joy.

Because of his genius, it is easy to forget that Parker earned his virtuosity through hours of listening and even more hours of practice. All over New York one could find graffiti saying, "Bird Lives." Experts such as Phil Schaap had a regular radio program on WKCR called "Bird Flight" in which every measure, every breath, every performance of Parker were painstakingly analyzed.[23] There is great energy, no wasted space, no saccharine melodic forays in his music. It is, as Gioia puts it, "a purer conception of jazz: an art music with the emotional pungency of a battle cry."[24]

Parker has been compared to Jackson Pollock and Orson Welles. He embodied both the angst and the quest for freedom of his generation. Not every bebop musician was as troubled as was he, but, in his anguish, he was not only the embodiment of the postwar generation, he was in many ways ahead of his time. As Richard Brody elegantly puts it, "Parker's drive toward perpetual revolution in ideas and styles, and in personal bearing, foreshadowed the history of jazz to come. And his martyrdom to an art of self-revelation, demonstration, defiance, and revolt foreshadowed the tragic heroism of a generation of civil rights leaders to come."[25]

Finally, we come to one of the most complex figures in jazz: Miles Dewey Davis III (1926–1991). Though strongly involved in bebop to begin with, Davis eventually moved into something of a new way of playing it, sometimes called "cool." Whereas Dizzy and Bird, along with so many others, played complex improvisations over generally unrelenting rhythm sections, much of Miles's music, which began as "hard bop," became more subtle and impressionistic, emphasizing timbre. His family moved to East St. Louis, where the Davises lived, and then he moved to New York in 1944. Historians believe that the city of St. Louis had a formative influence on

---

[23]"Phil Schaap WKCR Radio Archives," Phil Schaap Jazz, www.philschaapjazz.com/index .php?l=page_view&p=radio.

[24]Ted Gioia, *History of Jazz*, 209.

[25]Richard Brody, "How Charlie Parker Defined the Sound and Substance of Bebop Jazz," The Front Row, *New Yorker*, August 29, 2020, www.newyorker.com/culture/the-front-row /how-charlie-parker-defined-the-sound-and-substance-of-bebop-jazz/.

the young Miles. He cut his teeth in various bands, guided by trumpet teachers. According to Eugene Redmond, "Miles Davis is emblematic of East St. Louis. He symbolizes East St. Louis. He actualizes East St. Louis."[26]

Figure 10.1. Miles Davis could be critical of fellow jazz musicians, but with recordings such as *Birth of the Cool* and *Kind of Blue*, he exhibits his "cool jazz" style.

Miles was famously prickly and announced critical views of his fellow musicians: Oscar Peterson couldn't play the blues; McCoy Tyner, the pianist, couldn't play a note; West Coast jazz was skillful but monotonous; Dave Brubeck had great harmonies but couldn't swing; and the like.[27] He often

[26]Eugene B. Redmond, "'So What' (?) . . . It's 'All Blues' Anyway: An Anecdotal/Jazzological Tour of Milesville," in *Miles Davis and American Culture*, ed. Gerald Early (St. Louis: Missouri Historical Society Press, 2001), 55.
[27]These views are spread throughout two volumes: Miles Davis and Quincy Troupe, *Miles Davis: The Autobiography* (New York: Simon & Schuster, 1989) 69, 141, 236; and *Miles on*

played with his back to the audience and was known to be abusive to women and to struggle with heroin. Paradoxically, Davis was shy, often admiring of White musicians, and complementary of greats, such as Coleman Hawkins, Ahmad Jamal, and the blues singer Bessie Smith. It took me some time to become reconciled with his coldness and still recognize the genius of the music.

In the 1950s he began to develop his signature style. He used the mute a good deal and incorporated long legato melodic lines. It might be said that he was as good at setting an atmosphere as he was at selecting the notes. The technical word for what he was doing is timbre, a term meaning "tone color." It has more to do with the mood than pitch or dynamics. Miles, better than most, could set a mood in a song. Sometimes a single piece could last forty-five minutes. Davis often walked around the stage, pausing at each musician's post, as it were, urging them on.[28]

On his album *Milestones* (1958) he explored modal sounds, departing from the strictly diatonic (white notes) conventions of earlier jazz.[29] In the sequel, *Kind of Blue* (1959), he recorded with an astonishing cast of all stars: John Coltrane and Julian "Cannonball" Adderley (saxophones), Bill Evans (piano), Paul Chambers (bass), Jimmy Cobb (percussion), and the relatively unknown Wynton Kelly (one track on piano). Here the music is even further from hard bop, becoming fully modal. The result is considered one of the great masterpieces of jazz history.[30]

Miles was always moving musically. He surrounded himself with new and talented musicians. He entered his "electric period," using elements from rock and fusion. He broke off with music for several years, but he then staged a remarkable comeback, and he became more socially active, helping combat apartheid in South Africa before dying of a brain hemorrhage in 1991, aged sixty-five.

Miles: Interviews and Encounters with Miles Davis, ed. Paul Maher Jr. and Michael K. Dorr (Toronto: Lawrence Hill, 2008).

[28]See *Miles in Paris, 1989*: www.youtube.com/watch?v=xVcd6PV8TpA.

[29]"Miles Davis - Dr. Jackle," YouTube video, 5:50, posted by "JazzTuna," December 17, 2011, www.youtube.com/watch?v=QHk9Cgqa3yI.

[30]"M I L E S D A V I S - Kind Of Blue - Full Album," YouTube video, 1:18:05, posted by "Jazz Night," August 2, 2021, www.youtube.com/watch?v=vDqULFUg6CY.

What is Davis's legacy, and how has his music contributed to the aesthetics of jazz? Perhaps this is best summed up in the words of Christopher Smith: "Miles Davis' artistic interest was in the creation and manipulation of ritual space, in which gestures could be endowed with symbolic power sufficient to form a functional communicative, and hence musical, vocabulary."[31] This creation is deeply indebted to African American tradition, but it also shows the ability of jazz to incorporate many elements from the outside world. Davis could incorporate elements from rock music to Spanish and African roots. Rather than closing one chapter and opening another, he built on his past.[32] This capacity of jazz to integrate components of various styles and traditions dates back to the early masters, beginning at least with Duke Ellington. This testifies to the vivacity of jazz, and it partly explains why different musicians were uncomfortable with the term *jazz* to describe their work.

Bebop and cool remain two of the great expressions of jazz. There was both continuity and discontinuity with older versions, but as with all forms of jazz, a movement from deep sorrow to inextinguishable joy is all over the music.

---

[31]Christopher Smith, "A Sense of the Possible: Miles Davis and the Semiotics of Improvised Performance," *TDR* 39, no. 3 (1995): 41.

[32]See Paul Tingen, "How Miles Davis Put Together the Greatest Rock 'n' Roll Band You Ever Heard," *Jazzwise* (November 2003), www.jazzwise.com/features/article/how-miles-davis -put-together-the-greatest-rock-n-roll-band-you-ever-heard/.

11

GOSPEL IN JAZZ

THE CHRISTIAN MESSAGE
IN THE MUSICIANS
AND THE MUSIC

Jazz musicians, even agnostic ones, have a soft spot
for gospel. It's part of the foundation of American music,
an essential language like the blues.

TOM MOON

If it is true, as Moon claims, that all jazz musicians have a "soft spot" for gospel, then it is also the case that this is more evident in the work of some artists than others. In the songs and playing of some jazz musicians, you hear gospel. This may be in small allusions here and there, or it may be in the overall deference toward a gospel sound. Saxophonist Kirk Whalum is quite intentional about the connection. More often, though, it is simply a hint, such as the way a pianist might structure the chords or a call-and-response pattern. This connection should not surprise us, of course, considering that so many musicians began in the church.

And yet I believe that there is more to it. Indeed, I argue that the entire musical genre that is jazz is best heard as a reflection not just of a certain gospel sound, but as a musical echo of the good news of Christ. In this chapter, then, I will briefly look at a few of the most prominent jazz musicians who have shown such a "soft spot."

Figure 11.1. Jamaican musician Monty Alexander reflects the influence of gospel music on jazz while also incorporating new sounds into the genre.

Sister Rosetta Tharpe (1915–1973) had a burden to bring gospel into the highways and byways. In that manner, she could not have been more different from Mahalia Jackson, who believed gospel should stay in the church, or at least be greeted with an aura of worshipful reverence. Born into a musical family, Tharpe grew up in the Church of God in Christ, a denomination founded by Charles Harrison Mason, a Black Pentecostal with a conviction that church music should be rhythmical, lively, and winsome. Tharpe became an adept guitar player and is said to have introduced the electric guitar into public performance. She was even dubbed the "godmother of rock-and-roll."[1] In 1938, she left the church circuit and went into show business, arguing that people in nightclubs needed the gospel as much as anyone. Naturally, she was criticized for this attitude by purists, yet she persisted. Perhaps her moment of greatest triumph was in Great Britain, where she gave numerous concerts and earned accolades from Eric Clapton, Jeff Beck, and Keith Richards.[2]

---

[1]See Gayle Wilde, *Shout, Sister, Shout: The Untold Story of Rock-and-Roll Trailblazer Sister Rosetta Tharpe* (Boston: Beacon, 2007), xi.

[2]See the footage of gospel classics "Didn't It Rain" and "Trouble in Mind" in Manchester, England: "Sister Rosetta Tharpe – Didn't It Rain-Live In Manchester, England 1964," YouTube video, 6:48, posted by "Mike Bizimis," December 28, 2015, www.youtube.com /watch?v=jGPx4ancGhg.

Unlike Sister Rosetta, most jazz musicians did not make gospel the main feature of their music. Yet many have seen fit to unite gospel to their own styles, and often to great effect. One of the most remarkable examples is Duke Ellington. Throughout his career, he respected African American religious music, and at times he focused on it. Perhaps his most powerful gospel song is "Come Sunday." It first appeared in a Carnegie Hall concert within an extended piece called *Black, Brown and Beige*, discussed previously. Jazz musicians of all stripes include it in their repertoire, but most have no idea of its provenance. The lyrics were added later, possibly cowritten by Mahalia Jackson:

Lord, dear Lord of love,

God almighty,

God above,

Please look down and see my people through.

I believe the sun and moon

Will shine up in the sky

When the day is gray,

I know it, clouds passing by . . .

He'll give peace and comfort

To every troubled mind

Come Sunday, come Sunday, that's the day.[3]

In the last decades of his life, Duke wrote three sacred concerts. He considered these the most significant part of his œuvre.[4] They were performed in Grace Cathedral, San Francisco, Saint John the Divine in New

---

[3]From his Sacred Concerts, with Mahalia Jackson: "Come Sunday - Mahalia Jackson," YouTube video, 5:48, posted by "bill K," January 14, 2012, www.youtube.com/watch?v =x0PlS8nuceA.

[4]See Janna Tull Steed, *Duke Ellington: A Spiritual Biography* (Chestnut Ridge, NY: Crossroad, 1999).

York, and Westminster Abbey in London. Songs, besides "Come Sunday" in its several guises, included the magnificent "In the Beginning, God," "The Lord's Prayer," "Heaven," and "The Shepherd." This last piece was dedicated to John G. Gensel, the legendary "jazz pastor" of St. Peter's Church in New York.

Another, quite different, jazz musician who wrote sacred music was Mary Lou Williams (1910–1981). She was a child prodigy. Early on she experienced racism; White neighbors threw bricks into her windows— until she started to play at their homes. She became a professional musician at age fifteen, citing Lovie Austin as her model. Austin was a band leader and was considered, along with Lil Hardin Armstrong, to be the greatest female jazz musician of the 1920s. Benny Goodman promoted Williams and commissioned blues numbers from her. One of them, "Roll 'Em," became a Goodman signature song. She also wrote the "Camel Hop," named for the cigarette company that sponsored Goodman. In 1956, she converted from being Baptist to Roman Catholic, took a break from music, and dedicated her life to helping musicians with addictions. When she returned to her music career, she focused on writing music for the liturgy. Her gospel masterpiece is no doubt the jazz mass *Saint Martin of Porres*, in honor of the patron saint of Peru and subtitled, "A Celebration of the Black Messiah of the Andes."[5] Written in 1962, it was the first of several sacred pieces she composed in her last decades. Her close harmonies and jazz-like melodies translate into truly powerful music.

CELEBRATING FREEDOM

It should come as no surprise that many musicians, Black and White, celebrated freedom. As discussed at length, that was a conviction and a hope born out of the Black experience. This sensibility clearly has affinities with the biblical idea of emancipation (Rom 8:1-20). The anniversary of Juneteenth, now a national holiday, has always been accompanied by the narrative of jazz music. Though emancipation was

---

[5]"St. Martin de Porres," YouTube video, 6:36, posted by "Mary Lou Williams – Topic," May 21, 2015, www.youtube.com/watch?v=I_LcpXEA0W4.

officially declared January 1, 1863, it took time before freedom could become a reality, if it has. On June 19, 1865, with the Confederate forces having surrendered, Union soldiers arrived in Galveston, Texas, spreading the news of the end of the war. The date, some two and a half years after official emancipation, became a metaphor for the newly minted freedom: declared but unrealized. *General Order Number 3* is a moving piece of legislation:

> The people of Texas are informed that in accordance with a proclamation from the Executive of the United States, all slaves are free. This involves an absolute equality of rights and rights of property between former masters and slaves, and the connection heretofore existing between them becomes that between employer and hired laborer.

As can be imagined, the reactions to this statement ranged from great joy to shock and anger. Well over a century and a half later, much of the content of this proclamation has not been fully absorbed. Ralph Ellison's posthumous novel *Juneteenth* contains many of the great poet's thoughts about life and music. Jazz was for him the embodiment of what it means to be human: "But what a feeling can come over a man just from seeing the things he believes in and hopes for symbolized in the concrete form of a man. In something that gives a focus to all the other things he knows to be real. Something that makes unseen things manifest and allows him to come to his hopes and dreams through his outer eye and through the touch and feel of his natural hand."[6]

Several composers have written fairly substantial works that, I would argue, qualify as gospel in a jazz mode. One of the most impressive is Wynton Marsalis's *Abyssinian Mass*.[7] He wrote it in 2008 as a celebration of the two hundredth anniversary of the Abyssinian Baptist Church in

---

[6]Ralph Ellison, *Juneteenth* (New York: Vintage Books, 2021), 278.
[7]The complete premier is available, conducted by Damien Sneed: "Devotional (feat. Damien Sneed and Chorale Le Chateau)," YouTube video, 8:33, posted by "Jazz at Lincoln Center Orchestra – Topic," March 17, 2016, www.youtube.com/watch?v=7z3luZR9Gqs&list=PLG2 IqYdWFjPBUseTHilnmCoS_zUss1fER.

Harlem. With a running time of over two hours, it exhibits various styles from the African American tradition, all organized under the rubric of the traditional mass. A number of the segments directly appeal to freedom: "We Are on Our Way" and "Come and Join the Army" are powerful calls to emancipation. Particularly moving is the rendition of "The Lord's Prayer," which in its own way is an ode to liberty.

Pianist and educator Billy Taylor wrote a suite titled *Let Us Make a Joyful Noise to the Lord*. The title song has been recorded several times, including with a large choir from the Riverside Church in New York.[8] The full suite includes marvelous pieces such as "Spiritual," "Rejoice," "Prayer," "Celebrate," and "Walking in the Light." In my jazz band, we particularly enjoy playing "Prayer," so full of Taylor's rich harmonies. These pieces exude the spirit of emancipation and joy found in gospel music. As we have argued, the kind of joy embodied in the music is not superficial happiness, but the kind of joy found in the New Testament, where it is conjoined with refinement and suffering. As the apostle James puts it, "Count it all joy, my brothers, when you meet trials of various kinds, for you know that the testing of your faith produces steadfastness. And let steadfastness have its full effect, that you may be perfect and complete, lacking in nothing" (Jas 1:2-3).

No doubt Taylor's most well-known spiritual song is "I Wish I Knew How It Would Feel to Be Free." The theme of freedom is resplendent throughout jazz music. No version of it is more passionate than that of civil rights advocate Nina Simone.[9] Spiritual-like, the song is an appeal for freedom; it expresses the frustration and anger of an oppressed people:

Then you'd see I wish I knew how it would feel to be free

I wish I could break

---

[8]"Let Us Make a Joyful Noise Unto The Lord (Billy Taylor)," YouTube video, 4:28, posted by "The Riverside Church," November 20, 2018, www.youtube.com/watch?v=OQJ57gcR0 qk&t=90s.

[9]"Nina Simone - I Wish I Knew How It Would Feel to Be Free (Official Audio)," YouTube video, 3:10, posted by "Nina Simone," November 4, 2016, www.youtube.com/watch?v =inNBpizpZkE.

All the chains holdin' me

I wish I could say

All the things that I should say

Say 'em loud, say 'em clear

For the whole 'round world to hear

I wish I could share

All the love that's in my heart

Remove all the thoughts

That keep us apart

I wish you could know

What it means to be me

and agree

That every man should be free.

In the same vein, Oscar Peterson has composed a "Hymn to Freedom," which is his ode to the civil rights movement. It also reflects the tradition of spirituals and is played by someone who obviously grew up in the church.[10]

When every heart joins every heart and together yearns for liberty

That's when we'll be free

When every hand joins every hand and together molds our destiny

That's when we'll be free

Any hour any day, the time soon will come when men will live in dignity

---

[10]"Oscar Peterson - Hymn To Freedom," YouTube video, 6:53, posted by "dgbailey777," December 13, 2010, www.youtube.com/watch?v=tCrrZ1NnCuM.

That's when we'll be free, we will be

When every man joins in our song and together singing harmony

That's when we'll be free.[11]

Another musician who is undeservedly ignored for his sacred works is Dave Brubeck. He once told me that he had written more sacred compositions than any other kind. His commitment to jazz as a vehicle for freedom is legendary: "Jazz stands for freedom," he once said. "It's supposed to be the voice of freedom: Get out there and improvise, and take chances, and don't be a perfectionist—leave that to the classical musicians."[12] As the performer of wildly popular tunes such as "Take Five" and "Blue Rondo à la Turk," Brubeck isn't known for his religious background, but it is quite vibrant. He was raised as a Presbyterian by a Christian Science mother who went to a Methodist church, but he eventually converted to Roman Catholicism. He tells people he has three favorite Jewish philosophers: Irving Goleman, Darius Milhaud, and Jesus Christ.[13] In 1979, he was commissioned to write a mass, and it is an extraordinary piece by any measure. His composition *To Hope! A Celebration* was written for a chorus and a brass quintet, plus organ, and a string ensemble. In addition to the standard elements of the mass, there are supplemental texts such as "The Desert and the Parched Land (Isaiah 35:1-4)," added by his wife, Iola.[14] Not all of Brubeck's sacred music is liturgical. One of my favorite "religious" pieces from him is "Pilgrim's Progress," a blues number that builds and builds, much like a believer on a journey. Originally named "Audrey," the title comes not so much from the epic by John Bunyan as it is a tribute to

[11]Oscar also wrote a beautiful Easter Suite: "Oscar Peterson Easter Suite," YouTube video, 4:29, posted by "tegoko," March 11, 2009, www.youtube.com/watch?v=LT59aiqEk0I.

[12]See "A Jazz Postmortem," *Chelsea News*, February 16, 2016, www.chelseanewsny.com /news/a-jazz-postmortem-NCNP1420010221302219997. There is a bit of irony here in that Brubeck drew on the music of classical composers such as Darius Milhaud.

[13]Matthew Brown, "The Religious Side of the Late Dave Brubeck and His Music," *Deseret News*, December 7, 2012, www.deseret.com/2012/12/7/20510823/the-religious-side-of-the -late-dave-brubeck-and-his-music/.

[14]"To Hope! A Celebration," YouTube video, 37:46, posted by "Boulder Chorale," July 21, 2016, www.youtube.com/watch?v=ZtfjhRo03m4.

one of his staff, Janet Pilgrim. But it also works as a metaphor for the Christian life.[15]

TRIBUTES TO SPIRITUALS

If the list of major religious works dedicated to freedom by jazz musicians is relatively easy to identify, the list of those who have taken a low-profile bow to sacred music is less so, though it is quite extensive. Here we can pinpoint some who have written individual songs that qualify as sacred and distinguish them (imperfectly) from many who have played individual spiritual numbers or even entire albums dedicated to sacred music. A brief reminder: the distinction of sacred and secular music (or anything else in life for that matter) is questionable. Is a love song secular? Not if you believe love is God's gift. Is the business world secular? Not if you believe the economic sphere is part of God's world. But just for the sake of convention, let's look at some of the protagonists of sacred music. Any list that highlights composers of specifically sacred songs is both extensible and, in this case, fairly subjective. So we will present a sampling, but one that should encourage the reader to examine them and then find their own preferences.

Pianist Hank Jones and bassist Charlie Haden have produced a marvelous album of spirituals and gospel, *Steal Away*. It contains fourteen songs from the spiritual or hymn tradition of Black folks. What strikes the listener is the simple, confident unshowy manner of their playing. In a word, the music has *soul*. This same duo has given us an immortal version of "Come Sunday."[16]

Two other pianists should come in for special mention. Cyrus Chestnut is perhaps the most innovative of today's younger pianists. Playing spirituals and hymns comes naturally to him as he was brought up in Mount Calvary Baptist Church in Baltimore. He studied at several prestigious

---

[15]"Dave Brubeck & Paul Desmond— Pilgrim's Progress," YouTube video, 9:20, posted by "kocn53," November 23, 2012, www.youtube.com/watch?v=BfeqaDa8Um8.

[16]"Come Sunday," YouTube video, 3:29, posted by "Charlie Haden – Topic," July 23, 2018, www.youtube.com/watch?v=yq9RBK0R2TI.

academies, including Peabody and Berklee, without losing his earthy touch, which often happens to talented young artists. Though he can keep up with the best of the standard players and bluesmen, his first love is clearly gospel. Some of his most prestigious albums are direct tributes to gospel, while others have a certain gospel feel to them.[17]

One of the brightest lights in jazz piano and an eclectic musician is Jamaican-born Monty Alexander. He is a strong believer but does not wear his religion on his sleeve. He did record an album of spirituals and hymns, *The River*, which contains a number of gospel songs, including his masterpiece, "Renewal," composed after a period of considerable struggle. It is a tone poem full of color and contrasts.[18]

Terrence Richburg thoughtfully reflected on the prospect of gospel jazz. He recognizes the fact that professing Christians are just as good as the best of musicians. But he also recognizes the historical connection between the gospel message and the marvelous music of jazz:

> Familiar names such as Jonathan Butler, John Patitucci, Kirk Whalum and many others are well-known as both top notch jazz artists and fervent believers. Some critics might label them as sell-outs to a type of secularism contradicting Christian principles and teachings. But the truth is Jazz is musical art, just as relevant as Classical, Gospel, Latin, African, Chinese, Japanese or any other style of music which has its heart rooted in experiential passion and cultural diversity.

He adds that jazz musicians should be uniquely poised to herald the biblical message of faith and trust in God:

> But I will go one step further to say that the improvisational element of both Jazz and Gospel render them the most precise conduits for rendering the kind of spontaneous praise to God referenced in

---

[17]"Jesus Loves Me," YouTube video, 3:53, posted by "Cyrus Chestnut – Topic," July 18, 2015, www.youtube.com/watch?v=QIOmlHkjUoY.

[18]"Renewal," YouTube video, 6:44, posted by "Monty Alexander – Topic," October 7, 2015, www.youtube.com/watch?v=t4GYA9TAGwI.

Psalm 150. There is also a breaking down of language barriers which allows Christian Jazz artists and musicians like no other messengers sent by God to reach those in that community who have not yet come to a point of belief in Christ.

Who better to minister to the lost in the world of Jazz than those who speak the vernacular understood by those listeners? Also, what truer testimony than a vessel created by God to give back to Him the gift of music received in a style that He alone has created and established for His own good pleasure and glory?[19]

The reasons for and the way in which jazz musicians adapt hymns and gospel to their work vary greatly. Many grew up on the church and want to acknowledge their tradition. Many find that gospel music says something their regular output does not, at least not in the same way. Some may have a message of sorts. For example, Charles Gayle, the remarkable saxophone and piano player, decided to live on the streets and intentionally be homeless. He did this in part to identify with a different kind of audience and in part to say something about the universality of jazz. Gayle considers his music to be "spiritual" and to lead people to the Lord in worship. He tries to relate it directly to the Old and New Testaments. The style is decidedly abstract and even free.[20]

Clarinetist and composer Don Byron plays in a variety of styles, including klezmer, inspired by his friendship with the Jewish community of South Bronx. He belongs to the Black Rock Coalition, a group that wants to promote African American music that is not simply the predictable music of Black folks typically promoted by Whites. His New Gospel Quintet explored the riches of southern gospel in the pursuit of world peace. Some exponents of gospel jazz are decidedly "smooth," and a listener might miss the earthiness of real gospel and authentic jazz. One of the best is Ben Tankard, a pastor and jazz

---

[19]"What Is Gospel Jazz?," Terrence Richburg, Terrence Richburg Webpage, https://terrenc erichburg.com/jazz-gospel-central.
[20]"Charles Gayle – Consecration," YouTube video, 1:07:25, posted by "Earthinspace 77," September 3, 2016, www.youtube.com/watch?v=5hU2zpTz7Dg.

pianist.[21] Instrumental groups like Bonfire play hymns and gospel music with a "new age" jazz beat.[22]

These and many other jazz musicians have explored the relationship between jazz and faith. Indeed, when I listen to jazz, I find that it possesses the ability to express precisely the kind of praise that the psalmist calls for:

Praise the LORD!
Praise God in his sanctuary;
   praise him in his mighty heavens!
Praise him for his mighty deeds;
   praise him according to his excellent greatness!
Praise him with trumpet sound;
   praise him with lute and harp!
Praise him with tambourine and dance;
   praise him with strings and pipe!
Praise him with sounding cymbals;
   praise him with loud clashing cymbals!
Let everything that has breath praise the LORD!
Praise the LORD! (Ps 150:1-6)

[21]"Ben Tankard – Heavenly Vibes," YouTube video, 4:03, posted by "1muzikfreek," November 11, 2010, www.youtube.com/watch?v=_Hr9fbqHpBM.

[22]"Gospel Jazz Music with Bonfire | Smooth Instrumental Gospel Jazz Songs Playlist Hi-Fi 2018," YouTube video, 1:02:26, posted by "The Relax Guys," June 7, 2018, www.youtube.com/watch?v=iVDX38lMgAk.

12

THE SPIRIT
OF JAZZ

JAZZ AND THE GOSPEL
MESSAGE

There is no question that jazz is still present in the culture,

but the larger question is: does jazz still matter?

GERALD EARLY AND INGRID MONSON

Village Voice **journalist** and Miles Davis's first wife, Frances Davis, wrote that his death "threatened to become a permanent void at the top of the bill" for jazz.[1] The loss of a defining leader in any field is always a challenge. Will there be a successor? Will the given institution completely change? Or will it die out? And, if it is still alive, what is the secret of its resilience? Stuart Nicholson's provocative book *Is Jazz Dead? (Or Has It Moved to a New Address)* argues that jazz will survive because it has gone global, and in doing so, it has brought out new local styles that are vital and ensure the future of this music.[2] I think that's true, but I also believe that there are other features that ensure jazz's resiliency. In particular, I would point to its ability to express the aesthetic of

---

[1]Francis Davis, "Like Young," *The Atlantic* (July 1996), https://www.theatlantic.com/magazine/archive/1996/07/like-young/376628/.

[2]Stuart Nicholson, *Is Jazz Dead? (Or Has It Moved to a New Address)* (New York: Routledge, 2005).

deep misery to inextinguishable joy that is common to the human experience and resonates with the Christian message.

OPPOSITES COEXIST

When our family lived in France, people would often ask the musicians with whom I played what style of jazz they performed. Many labeled it "middle jazz," meaning neither New Orleans nor modern. Such labels have some value, but very little. First, as we have seen, early jazz is more than strictly the New Orleans style, and, second, modern jazz is quite diverse. Indeed, if we go by Giddens and DeVeaux's periodization, the modern period extends to today and includes a great variety of styles. What meaningful trends, then, can we discern?

One trend that should not come as a surprise is the desire to connect clearly with historic jazz. Several factors contributed to this link to tradition. First and foremost is the significance of the music known as jazz to all generations. Thanks to the longevity of some of the musicians and the availability of recordings, we have access to its rich history. For example, when Louis Armstrong staged a comeback after a successful Town Hall concert in May 1947, he created a six-piece band comprising several jazz legends. Called the All Stars, for the next several decades they gave hundreds of performances per year and made many recordings. Pops appeared in some thirty films and the Broadway hit, *Hello, Dolly!*, singing a rendition of the theme song. This hit actually displaced the Beatles' tenure as the number one band on the Hot 100 list, where they had resided for three years. On May 9, 1964, *Hello Dolly!* bumped the rock group to second place. As we have noted, because Armstrong was a master of onstage antics, it is easy to misunderstand him, as many of his contemporaries did, as a sort of sell-out vaudevillian. However, as a musician, singer, and horn player, he was unsurpassed. It's no wonder that jazz musicians continue to imitate and revere him.

A more complex blending with the roots of jazz is found in the remarkable music of Wynton Marsalis. His enormous talent and high profile delving into jazz tradition has been internationally recognized.

Born in 1961, he came from a family full of musical ability. Eventually Wynton was entrusted with the artistic direction of jazz at Lincoln Center, which has drawn enormous attention to this music. Consider his album *Black Codes from the Underground*. The lead song begins with a stop-and-go modern sequence, and then moves into a bluesy swing sound.[3] In 2011, he collaborated with the legendary rock guitarist Eric Clapton to give an amazing concert, *Live from Lincoln Center*. The rollicking blues number "Corinna, Corinna" gives the sense of the sheer joy of a great musical collaboration, followed by an insightful discourse on the blues by Marsalis.[4]

Of course, mainstream jazz, from bebop to cool and beyond, continued. When it looked to some that this music might be on its last leg, some extraordinary talent emerged, doing more than keeping it alive. The Modern Jazz Quartet featured the brilliant pianist-composer John Lewis, the unsurpassed vibraphonist Milt Jackson, percussionist Kenny Clarke, and the irrepressible Ray Brown on bass. Their masterpiece is undoubtedly *Django*, a kind of classical-sounding, bluesy jazz sonata.[5]

Some White musicians rose to prominence as well. Dave Brubeck, mentioned earlier, brought his imaginative rhythms to jazz, and pieces such as "Take Five" are still considered standards. Stan Getz was known for his wispy, lush sound on the tenor saxophone. He will especially be remembered for his forays into Brazilian rhythms, including his unforgettable joint album with João Gilberto, *Getz/Gilberto* (1964). Gerry Mulligan played piano and baritone sax, and also composed and arranged tunes. He collaborated with many of the greats, including Miles Davis, Stan Kenton, and Claude Thornhill. The wonderful Jamaican musician Monty Alexander, to whom this book is lovingly dedicated, brought fresh sounds

---

[3]This version is played live at Ronnie Scott's, London's most prominent jazz club: "Black Codes - Wynton Marsalis Quintet at Ronnie Scott's 2013," YouTube video, 11:47, posted by "Wynton Marsalis," December 18, 2013, www.youtube.com/watch?v=7Z8ZTdDoDps.

[4]"Winton Marsalis Eric Clapton - Play the Blues 6/6," YouTube video, 9:33, posted by "Sebastián Quijano," September 19, 2013, www.youtube.com/watch?v=yhP6mPvdllc.

[5]"Modern Jazz Quartet - Django (HQ)," YouTube video, 7:05, posted by "Joel00123," May 14, 2013, www.youtube.com/watch?v=L4ksM27dVfs.

from the islands to jazz standards, and he continues to be both traditional and innovative to this day.

Other greats have emerged to bring a new perspective to jazz. Charles Mingus (1922–1979) was a giant by any measure. His talent on double bass was matched only by his gifts as composer and arranger. The titles of many of his numerous recordings are as imaginative as their content: *Pithecanthropus Erectus*, *Mingus Ah Um*, *The Black Saint and the Sinner Lady*, and so forth. His "Wednesday Night Prayer Meeting" puts you in the congregation. These musicians, among others, illustrate the point that, while they are rooted in jazz's main features, their music echoes something greater. It is not always a fully Christian outlook, but they often allude to jazz's undeniable Christian roots.

One jazz superstar from this era who must be highlighted is John Coltrane (1926–1967). He grew up in the church, though later he seemed to have become a universalist, believing all religions to be equivalent. He was driven, both as a musician and as a person. He began as a mostly bebop player but became increasingly modal. He practiced for hours and hours, perfecting his technique and learning to express lofty ideas in his music. As is well-known, in 1957, he experienced a transformation that delivered him from alcohol and drugs, and he subsequently gave credit to God: "By the grace of God, [I experienced] a spiritual awakening which was to lead me to a richer, fuller, more productive life. At that time, in gratitude, I humbly asked to be given the means and privilege to make others happy through music."[6] His music afterward was often in a spiritual genre. His *A Love Supreme* album remains an exceptional, even unparalleled, achievement.[7] The title of this book is a tribute to the piece. In his work, we see the evidence of both sorrow and personal struggle, as well as the joy of liberation and transformation that is only possible through God.

---

[6]John Coltrane, liner notes to *A Love Supreme*, Impulse! A-77, 1965, 33 1/3 rpm.
[7]"John Coltrane - A Love Supreme [Full Album] (1965)," YouTube video, 32:48, posted by "Jazzaddict 98," June 30, 2014, www.youtube.com/watch?v=ll3CMgiUPuU. See also Jamie Howison, *God's Mind in That Music* (Eugene, OR: Cascade Books, 2012).

Figure 12.1. With recordings such as *A Love Supreme,* saxophonist and composer John Coltrane achieved a kind of spirituality in his music.

I once had the privilege of hearing him play live with his famous quartet at the Jazz Workshop in Boston. And there I saw a man who had put his past behind him and was endeavoring to pursue a true spirituality. It would be too much to expect a doctrinally clear statement of evangelical faith. Some critics saw his transformation as pantheistic, but the reality is aesthetic and pious. Salim Washington offers one of the best summaries of Coltrane's achievements: "Coltrane's music was ultimately a meditation upon the joy and beauty that is possible in human life through knowledge and understanding of reality and devotion to goodness. His deep awareness of death and disappointment tempered his celebration through music, and retained the character of struggle that is necessary to gain real understanding of the fundamental conditions of human existence."[8]

---

[8]Salim Washington, "Meditations on Coltrane's Legacies," https://www.salimwashington .com/musings/meditations-on-coltranes-legacies.

FREE JAZZ–REALLY?

Almost at the opposite end of the spectrum within modern jazz, we have freestyle jazz. I will never forget purchasing and then playing, over and over again, John Coltrane's album *Giant Steps* (1960). The opener, "Ramblin'," is a blues tune that today sounds quite conventional, but at the time was strange, to say the least.[9] For one thing, Coleman played on a plastic sax (technically a Grafton, made from acrylic glass). But most remarkably, the solos took leaps and dives, and they were in fact the beginnings of a much more unbridled form that would appear in later decades. Even in his most free ventures, we are never too far from the melody or the basic chords.[10] This was not to everyone's liking, however. Critics of free jazz have accused it of departing so far from recognizable patterns that it should no longer qualify as jazz or even music. In my view this accusation might be true of radical free jazz, say of the Art Ensemble of Chicago, although even here there are some links to the sounds of jazz.[11] Cecil Taylor (1929–2018), who at best resembles Russian composer Alexander Scriabin, is another example, but sometimes his music sounds more like technically informed chaos.[12]

How should we understand free jazz? Perhaps it is a jazz equivalent of some of Pierre Boulez's most innovative music. In his formative years, Boulez (1925–2016) had all but denied that music had value before his radical serialism. In a nutshell, serial technique reduces entire pieces to "the series," a selection of twelve notes from the diatonic scale played forward and backward and in other combinations. He later recanted and admitted the value of Western music, even becoming conductor of the New York Philharmonic Orchestra. Interestingly, though a professed

---

[9]"Ornette Coleman – Ramblin'," YouTube video, 6:37, posted by "jazzhole13," February 9, 2010, www.youtube.com/watch?v=kqwdRBWvPs0.

[10]Consider Ornette Coleman, *Free Jazz: A Collective Improvisation*, recorded December 21, 1960, Atlantic SD 1364, 33⅓ rpm.

[11]"Art Ensemble of Chicago - Berlin Jazzfest - 1991 – Ohnedaruth," YouTube video, 19:02, posted by "Evil Monkeys," February 22, 2012, www.youtube.com/watch?v=z_U96i763zk.

[12]"Cecil Taylor - Free Improvisation #3," YouTube video, 10:08, posted by VegetativeHorse, January 8, 2010, www.youtube.com/watch?v=EstPgi4eMe4.

atheist, he wrote at least one quasi-liturgical work, *Rituel*. Similarly, even in the most groundbreaking forms of free jazz, there is something left of the traditional styles.[13] A number of historians consider it impossible to understand the emergence of free jazz without knowing the cultural ambiance. True, the musicians rebelled against conventional jazz struc- tures, but this paralleled a rebellion against the political structures of the day. Borrowing from Marxism, many of the musicians identified in jazz certain oppressive bourgeois values, and they felt it was time to protest them from within. Frank Kofasky says that free jazz signified a "vote of no confidence" in the American dream.[14] I think this is overstated. Jazz was never a stranger to the way-out sounds of atonality and avant-garde notions. Yet it retains all kinds of vestiges of traditional jazz. True, free jazz was nearly more of a socially conscious philosophical statement than pure music.

Yet there is music, even religious music, to be found in it for the per- sistent listener. It can be indirect. Without necessarily an explicit Christian confession, there are often various connections between a jazz perfor- mance and congregational worship, particularly in the African American tradition. Besides the bluesy way of singing or playing, there are the sense of increasing intensification; the call-and-response between the leader (soloist) and the assembly; and the invitation to engage the body with handclapping, dance, and nonverbal sounds.

WHAT JAZZ STILL DOES

As we have noted, social commentary and protest had been a feature of jazz from its beginnings. Of course, that can work both ways: both a cri- tique of the American dream and its defense. We have seen both. Protest against the system abound. But we don't want to neglect the other side.

---

[13]I had the privilege of studying with Pierre Boulez at Harvard in 1962. I also met Ornette Coleman in New York and was impressed by his kindness as well as his great knowledge of music. See his fascinating interviews: Jean Vermeil, *Conversations with Pierre Boulez: Thoughts on Conducting* (Blue Ridge Summit, PA: Amadeus, 2003).

[14]See Frank Kofsky, *Black Nationalism and Revolution in Music* (New York: Pantheon, 1970), 131.

During World War II, jazz was often seen as a music of resistance against Nazi hegemony. One humorous episode reveals the role of jazz under occupation. In the early 1940s, when Billie Holiday and others recorded the "St. Louis Blues," the Nazis objected because jazz was played by Black musicians. But the French producers explained the piece was a critique of the ancient monarchy (Saint Louis), and thus pro-socialist![15]

Figure 12.2. Singers such as Billie Holiday, known as "Lady Day," and musicians such as Nina Simone demonstrate the influence of female performers on jazz.

The Voice of America (VOA) featured jazz music along with its message of freedom. The VOA was established in 1942 as an organ of the United States government, and early on it was beamed on shortwave radio to scores of countries. Having spoken with many survivors of the war, I can

---

[15]Mike Zwerin, *La Tristesse de St Louis: Jazz Under the Nazis* (Sag Harbor, NY: Beech Tree Paperbacks, 1987).

say how important this voice was. Willis Conover hosted a daily jazz program from 1955 to 1996, featuring the greats from Louis Armstrong to Dizzy Gillespie and Duke Ellington. At its height the VOA jazz program was followed by over thirty million listeners. It continued in its role during the Cold War, and it could be that it was an important contributor to the fall of communism in 1989.

One of my favorite recent examples of social concern in jazz is that of Dominick Farinacci's *Modern Warrior*. Here various jazz musicians reflect on the plight of soldiers affected with posttraumatic stress disorder, bringing hope to thousands.[16] Another is Ruth Naomi Floyd's remarkable musical and poetic rendition of Frederick Douglass's life and times. Using quotes from his writing and correspondence, including a moving letter to Harriet Tubman, the offering reflects on the achievements and setbacks of freedom for Black people and for all people. In a public television presentation of Floyd's work, the reviewer asks the question: "Was Douglass a prophet?" And the answer comes forth, "Oh yes. He stayed close to the root. Didn't let the fruit deter him."[17]

FUSIONS

It has been argued that a major reason for the flourishing of jazz in the later twentieth and early twenty-first centuries is the music's ability to synthesize with styles and sounds from outside the mainstream. Of course, jazz has been married with other styles since its beginnings. As Ted Gioia writes, "Impure at its birth, jazz grew ever more so as it evolved. Its history is marked by a fondness for musical miscegenation, by its desire to couple with other styles and idioms, producing new, radically different progeny."[18] Let's look at some examples of these fusions and then consider whether this development is the key to the future of jazz. Three kinds of fusion

---

[16]"Modern Warrior Live at NatCon18," YouTube video, 19:41, posted by "National Council for Mental Wellbeing," May 10, 2018, www.youtube.com/watch?v=A6rGd2jf_W0.
[17]Chaz Howard, "Ruth Naomi Floyd, 'Frederick Douglass Jazz Works,' and Our Need for Free Critical Artists," WHYY (August 2, 2018), https://whyy.org/articles/ruth-naomi -floyd-frederick-douglass-jazz-works-and-our-need-for-free-critical-artists/.
[18]Ted Gioia, *The History of Jazz* (New York: Oxford University Press, 1997), 364.

have characterized jazz in the last decades of the twentieth and the first of the twenty-first centuries.

(1) The first example is jazz's fusion with rock music. Rock 'n' roll emerged in the 1950s, famously beginning with Bill Haley's "Rock Around the Clock" (1955), though of course it had earlier roots.[19] The rock-tinged album *Bitches Brew* (1970) made Miles Davis one of the pioneers of jazz-rock fusion. Though at first it seems to have little to do with the down-home pounding beats of rock, it clearly goes there.[20] This style became enormously popular with a young audience. Chick Corea became a household name, and the dynamic Weather Report, with the remarkable Joe Zawinul and Wayne Shorter, attracted fans of all kinds, almost re-writing the conventions of jazz. Their single "Birdland" had the effect of awakening the fanbase to a good old rhythm and blues sound, but with a distinctly modern feeling.[21]

Some rock fusion was more soul-oriented. One cannot deny the in-fluence of Jimi Hendrix on jazz. Sly Stone, James Brown, and even Frank Zappa played a role. And rock fusion could be artful as well as swinging: think of Greg Osby, Steve Coleman, Josh Redman, and the irrepressible Cassandra Wilson. Wilson by all accounts is an extraordinary musician. With her murky voice, she has fearlessly rendered the standards from the American song book, as well as spirituals, Robert Johnson's blues, pop music, and her own compositions. Other styles bespeak this fusion. The style known as acid jazz combines older roots with rap and hard bop. "Jestofunk" is full of rhythm, but in the most sophisticated way.[22]

(2) Jazz fusions have increasingly become international. The world music phenomenon has meant that boundaries and frontiers between

---

[19]As far back as 1914, Trixie Smith sang, "my man rocks me with one steady roll." See www.youtube.com/watch?v=PvzmBA9lP3c.

[20]"Miles Davis - Bitches Brew," YouTube video, 7:30, posted by "Julia Davila," February 6, 2010, www.youtube.com/watch?v=2AR93r-ASWI.

[21]"Birdland - Weather Report (1977)," YouTube video, 5:57, posted by "djbuddylovecooljazz," September 6, 2009, www.youtube.com/watch?v=vz7nMBLUnDc.

[22]"Acid Jazz Classics - Jazz Funk Soul Breaks Bossa Beats," YouTube video, 2:32:04, posted by "IRMA records Official," August 1, 2015, www.youtube.com/watch?v=S6l DGgs7jAc.

musicians and styles have collapsed. At the same time, local ethnic music has been a source of inspiration to jazz musicians. Of course, this has always been a characteristic of jazz. Dizzy Gillespie and others favored the Afro-Cuban influence on their music. Monty Alexander has found ways to combine jazz with the Island sounds of Jamaica. The bossa nova craze is still around, though perhaps less prominent than it was.

International fusions are where Stuart Nicholson believes the future of jazz is located. Music fusions, he argues, is a subset of globalization, which is an intensification of interaction in every sphere.[23] Of course, the flow moves both ways. A number of significant foreign-born musicians moved to the United States. One thinks of the prodigiously talented pianist Adam Makowitz coming to New York. But jazz is no longer only at home in New York, as one might have argued at one point. No, it is found in cities like Paris, London, Rome, and in countries such as Australia, Japan, and Norway. In each case, there is adaptation, much is the way a language is adapted into different shapes as it merges into a new culture.[24] Another example, among many, of artists who fuse traditional jazz with local elements is Mulatu Astatke. He trained in England and New York, but he kept his Ethiopian roots. Having played with Duke Ellington before Haile Selassie, he loves the great tradition of American jazz. Yet he labels his music "Ethio Jazz." He notes that this style is about "freedom in music."[25]

It may be too much to believe the actual survival of jazz is thanks to these global fusions. It is more likely, as E. Taylor Atkins once said, that "[jazz] enabled a rediscovery, redefinition or renewed expression of local traditions which were then marshaled to broaden and transform the music's expressive capacities."[26] But just what are the music's expressive

---

[23]Nicholson, *Is Jazz Dead?*, 164-66.
[24]Nicholson, *Is Jazz Dead?*, 173. Nicholson makes considerable use of the concept of "glocalization." Nicholson seems particularly enamored with Norwegian jazz, focusing on musicians such as Bugge Wesseltoft and Nils Petter Molvaer: Nicholson, *Is Jazz Dead?*, 146-53, 202-8.
[25]David Pilling, "Jazz Pioneer Mulatu Astatke: 'All I Do Is Play My Music'," *Financial Times*, September 3, 2021, www.ft.com/content/8a3a97ad-7dfd-406e-92c4-ca930e8c78d1.
[26]Stuart Nicholson, *Is Jazz Dead?*, 226.

capacities? I believe that it bespeaks a narrative that moves from deep misery to inexpressible joy, using the major qualities of African American musical expression, improvisation, call-and-response, swing, and so on. This narrative, which reflects the complexities of the human experience—our pain, our struggles, our hopes, our joys—is not bound to one time or culture. Rather, like the Christian message with which it is closely aligned, it reaches across cultural contexts, geographical borders, and musical styles.

(3) Fusions between jazz and classical music have also occurred. There had always been some cross-fertilization between jazz and classical music. In the early days "legit" composers such as Igor Stravinsky, Maurice Ravel, Darius Milhaud, and Aaron Copeland integrated elements of jazz into their own compositions. Stravinsky composed his *Ragtime for 11 Instruments* in 1918. Ravel had several pieces in a jazz mode, including Sonata Number 2 for Violin and Piano (1927), and, of course, his Concerto for Left Hand (1931). Milhaud used jazz in his *La création du monde* (1923). Copeland often integrated jazz into his music, including the Concerto for Piano and Orchestra (1926).

Such fusions stressed the formal aspects of jazz. In more recent times, improvisation has become the focus. An outstanding example is the ECM record label, led by Manfred Eicher and his colleagues, beginning in 1969. It has produced many extraordinary musicians, many of them trained in classical music, but then showing themselves especially adept at jazz. Perhaps the best-known of these is the somewhat eccentric pianist Keith Jarrett. Originally from Allentown, Pennsylvania, Jarrett (b. 1945) is world famous today. His *Köln Concert* (1975) became one of the bestselling albums of all time. It is a long solo piano rendition with tremendous variety, great bursts of musical energy, and an eclectic combination of classical, jazz, gospel, and rock.[27] Then there is the stunning Bobby McFerrin. A vocalist, a composer, and a conductor, he has interacted with

---

[27]"Keith Jarrett - THE KÖLN CONCERT - complete, Tomasz Trzcinski – piano," YouTube video, 1:11:10, posted by "Tomasz Trzcinski," August 7, 2014, www.youtube.com/watch?v =T_IWlwLZhzE.

most every kind of style. His vocals are unpredictable, using a straight voice, but venturing into falsetto, whistles, and scat, and he is notable for inviting audience participation. One of the great moments in music history is his collaboration with the astounding cellist Yo-Yo Ma.[28] The group Oregon, whose use of the oboe is particularly striking, is another to have emerged from this label's promotion.[29] Vibraphonist Gary Burton and Chick Corea have often collaborated to produce a unique sound, as can be heard in "Armando's Rumba."[30]

To my mind, the numerous ways that jazz has been adapted to different cultures and fused with different musical styles to create new sounds and genres reminds me of the adaptation of the Christian gospel to different cultures, languages, and geographies across time. Like jazz, the message of Christ's life, death, and resurrection came out of a particular set of historical events and circumstances, but it was not meant for one people, but for the whole world. The appeal of jazz across such boundaries is, for me, another example of the resonance between jazz and faith.

THE ISSUE OF MACHINERY

Along with these combinations, jazz grew in unique ways through certain technologies. From the beginnings of jazz, sound systems have lent support to performances. Musicians are often rightly demanding about them. Of course, if you can afford it, having your own trusted team of sound engineers come with you and spend time doing extensive sound-checks is a great benefit. Sometimes the sound system can be overdone. There is a legend about a concert that Count Basie gave at the Nice Jazz Festival. In the middle of one of the pieces, all the lights went out and so did the amplification. But the band kept playing. When the electricity

[28]"Yo-Yo Ma & Bobby McFerrin," YouTube video, 2:46, posted by "liou1982," May 8, 2007, www.youtube.com/watch?v=GczSTQ2nv94.

[29]Listen to them at the Catania Festival: "Oregon - Catania Jazz, 20 marzo 2018 – ABC," YouTube video, 1:25:07, posted by "Francesco Restuccia," March 29, 2018, www.youtube.com/watch?v=7jhb1j13iCE.

[30]"Chick Corea & Gary Burton - Armando's Rumba," YouTube video, 5:07, posted by "uvisniyellow," October 3, 2011, www.youtube.com/watch?v=VRSjLkj0VMw.

came back on the audience booed! The unsupported sound of the orchestra was so pure and so clean that they wanted it back.

A word about stage maneuvers might be in order. There has been a friendly controversy between jazz purists and rock stars over the advantages of stage devices such as smoke and fog, loud percussion, and special effects in performances. Many complain that the trend from "song to spectacle" is unhealthy, and I would agree that much of it is. But a judicious use of technology can be as much of an art form as a purely acoustical performance. Take for instance the introduction of the Hammond B3 organ to jazz. The organ has been around for a long time, particularly in the church, though its introduction in the church was a controversy at the time. Fats Waller and Count Basie both used the Estey organ, and Wild Bill Davis began to use the Hammond in 1949. The king of the instrument is no doubt Jimmy Smith, whose *Who's Afraid of Virginia Woolf?* is unsurpassed.[31]

As with nearly every area of life, the use of some form of technology is inevitable within music. The same could even be said of Christianity, which has throughout its history employed technologies as varied as ancient road systems, printing presses, radio and television, and current forms of social media to share the good news. The question is how one may use technology in a way that is consistent with and faithful to the message.

JAZZ AND THE SPIRIT

So, does jazz still matter? The authors of the epigraph above answer their own question in the affirmative, and I will add my "amen" to that. Yes, jazz still matters. One reason, drawing attention to one of its fundamental features, is the enduring nature of its type of improvisation: "We think [jazz] does [matter] in ways that are rather astonishing. . . . We suggest that jazz improvisation remains a compelling metaphor for inter-relationship, group creativity, and freedom that is both aesthetic and

---

[31]"Jimmy Smith - Who's Afraid of Virginia Wolf (1964)," YouTube video, 4:58, posted by "Bob Hardy," February 6, 2008, www.youtube.com/watch?v=CG0r803mKPI. See also a talented young Hammond B3 musician, Matthew Whitaker: "jazzahead! 2019 - Matthew Whitaker," YouTube video, 45:43, posted by "jazzaheadtradefair," April 27, 2019, www.youtube.com /watch?v=oKEZ3CgygF8.

social."[32] This technical feature of jazz means that it, more than perhaps any other form of music, is open to new insights, sounds, and artistic creations.

Of course, jazz's durability is due to more than this. At the risk of sounding like a bromide, it is my conviction that few forms of music compare to jazz as a metaphor for life. In light of its historical roots and the message contained within, it embodies the vagaries of human life and the movement from sorrow to joy. One of the best summaries is from a somewhat obscure minister, Alvin L. Kershaw, who made his name appearing on the old *The $64,000 Question* television program and then donating his winnings to the National Association for the Advancement of Colored People. But he was a considerable expert on jazz in his day, hosting jazz events and becoming friends with many jazz musicians, including Dizzy Gillespie.[33] He wrote:

> Jazz helps us be sensitive to the whole range of existence. Far from offering us rose-colored glasses . . . it realistically speaks of sorrow and pain . . . it helps us relate and interpret the variety of experiences we have had. . . . Jazz stimulates us to feel deeply and truthfully. . . . Jazz thunders a mighty "yes." . . . It offers us an urgency to live fully.[34]

This clearly resonates with my claim that jazz moves us from deep misery to inextinguishable joy! Interestingly, Kershaw added that jazz could be more of an act of worship for him than the singing of many traditional hymns.

But my added conviction is that this movement within jazz can only be properly understood when heard in light of the gospel of Jesus Christ, in which our collective human misery—our separation from God—is overcome through the painful death and victorious, joyful resurrection

---

[32]Gerald Early & Ingrid Monson, "Why Jazz Still Matters," *Dædalus*, Spring 2019, 10.

[33]"Archives: Music," Emmanuel Church in the city of Boston website, www.emmanuelboston .org/tag/music/.

[34]Quoted in Marshall W. Stearns, *The Story of Jazz* (New York: Oxford University Press, 1956), 304.

of Christ. When we hear jazz through the mysterious movement of the
Holy Spirit, we can begin to perceive the love of God, which addresses our
human needs that are so painfully and wonderfully embodied in jazz.

Of course, relating jazz to the movement of the Spirit rests on much
more than the faith of individual musicians, important as that may be. It
is true, as we have seen, that there have been many jazz musicians who
are committed believers. We have mentioned a few of them: King Oliver,
Duke Ellington, Cyrus Chestnut, Monty Alexander, Hank Jones, Mary
Lou Williams, Dave Brubeck, and a host of others. In addition, there are
musicians who are "spiritually" dedicated, though not necessarily as or-
thodox Christians. John Coltrane and Don Byron come to mind. And
then there are many who have composed and performed gospel music:
Billy Taylor, Charles Mingus, Oscar Peterson, Keith Jarrett, and many
others. But my point here is that there is a far deeper connection of jazz
and the Spirit than can be traced to individuals. There is something about
the music itself that is profoundly connected to the truths about life and
the truth found in the Christian message.

Returning to Ted Gioia's remark about jazz being both entertaining
and innovative, he adds that this relates to yet another paradox—namely,
that the most progressive attitude derived from players who came from
America's most disempowered underclass.[35] Recognizing this paradox
leads us to avow that jazz, at its best, not only redresses an imbalance, be
it injustice or suffering, but affirms a positive sound, the sound of freedom
and integrity. Such a statement sounds vague, but there are many contours
of this characteristic.

A first contour that animates the paradox of jazz is *suffering*. Like Jesus
himself, so many Black folks have been acquainted with grief, suffering,
betrayal, and pain. It would be unthinkable for Black music not to reflect
this. Songs can convey sorrow in a way few other artistic media can. The
lament for a deceased woman at the St. James Infirmary Hospital known
as the "St. James Infirmary Blues," which has been performed by many,

---

[35]Ted Gioia, *History of Jazz*, 200.

including Louis Armstrong, Cab Calloway, and Bobby "Blue" Bland, is heartbreaking. A certain amount of mystery surrounds the origins of the song. It may have been based on an old English folk song, "The Unfortunate Rake." The sex of the victim is ambiguous, for this song is also known as the "Gambler's Blues" about a man who wasted his life on high living. In any case, the song is stark, sad, and seemingly without hope. The suffering here, as in so much of jazz, is agonizing.[36]

A second, related contour is *protest*. As we have noted, there are unhealthy forms of protest, but there are also salutary—even necessary—ones. The list of musicians who embedded social protest in their music is extensive. James Reese Europe, who was especially popular in France in the early twentieth century, comes to mind. He hoped to use his international fame as a platform for seeking racial justice.[37] Louis Armstrong, Duke Ellington, Billie Holiday, and Charles Mingus all brought a degree of civil awareness to jazz fans. A redoubtable force in social awareness was the unparalleled Nina Simone. She grew up in the church, and her songs, like "Feeling Good" and "I Wish I Knew How It Would Feel to Be Free," often carry a prophet-like disgust at injustice. She was so angered by the murder of Medgar Evers that she sang a powerful, even frightening, song about Mississippi in which she said she even ceased to believe in prayer.[38] Perhaps this is how Isaiah, Jeremiah, Micah, or Amos would have sounded as musicians. Jazz and the quest for justice often go together. And this quest can be documented as a constant battle for recognition against a dominant culture that was patently racist.[39]

---

[36]Bobby "Blue" Bland sings it powerfully: "Bobby Bland - St James Infirmary," YouTube video, 3:11, posted by "shortrax," July 19, 2008, www.youtube.com/watch?v=iHh4 wBGQZD0.

[37]"World War I and Postwar Society," The African American Odyssey: A Quest for Full Citizenship: World, online exhibit, Library of Congress, www.loc.gov/exhibits/african -american-odyssey/world-war-i-and-postwar-society.html.

[38]"Nina Simone: Mississippi Goddam," YouTube video, 4:40, posted by "Aaron Overfield," February 26, 2013, www.youtube.com/watch?v=LJ25-U3jNWM.

[39]See Gerald Horne, *Jazz and Justice: Racism and the Political Economy of the Music* (New York: Monthly Review Press, 2019), 109-16.

Finally, though, there is *joy* to be found at the end of the road. It is hard-won and costly, yet the joy is real. Far beyond an earthly happiness, the good news of Jesus Christ is the source of a lasting joy. It was that good news, embodied in the Black church and reflected in Black music, especially jazz, that brought enslaved Africans into a place of freedom and that continues to reach people of all cultures and races. Jazz and the Spirit—not just the spirit of music, but the Holy Spirit—are profoundly interwoven.[40]

So, I say again, yes, jazz still matters. Its future is assured by many factors: different styles, fusions, and a global setting. Most importantly, though, jazz matters because it is a metaphor of life. It reflects our human condition, and it would not be what it is without the inspiration of the gospel. The music of jazz might lead one to cry, to lament, or to protest. But, deep in its roots, it also leads one to worship of God.

---

[40]Frank A. Salamone, *The Culture of Jazz: Jazz as Critical Culture* (Lanham, MD: University Press of America, 2009), 120-28.

13

THE GLORIES OF JAZZ

WHAT'S NOT TO LOVE?

There is no greater love
Than what I feel for you.

ISHAM JONES

T his chapter will probably appear more personal than the previous ones. Yet it emerges from them, and I hope will convince readers of the joys and glories of this extraordinary music we call jazz.

JAZZ AS CULTURE

What is jazz? Not all jazz artists like the label, as we have seen. Duke Ellington thought it was racist, a way of pigeonholing Black people according to a particular genre and keeping them from the canons of great music. But for convenience, we will use this label and hope the reader understands the problems. Let's add to the list of definitions that we have already considered this one by Burton W. Peretti: "Jazz, born through migration to New Orleans, can be defined as instrumental blues, featuring individual and collective improvisation and a unique 'swinging' of the beat."[1]

---

[1] Burton W. Peretti, *The Creation of Jazz: Music, Race and Culture in Urban America* (Urbana: University of Illinois Press, 1992), 21.

As Peretti points out, jazz, like any kind of music, was born out of a particular context and history—in this case, the suffering and pain of Black people, which deeply informed both earlier musical genres and the development of jazz itself. And, like other kinds of music, jazz is studded with unique figures. Buddy Bolden was mentally ill. Jelly Roll Morton had delusions of grandeur. Artie Shaw felt persecuted as a Jewish musician. King Oliver placed a handkerchief over his fingers so no one could copy his trumpet solos. Charles Mingus got into barroom brawls. Keith Jarrett called for a piano tuner in front of three hundred people.

But it has been the argument of this book that jazz, in all its diversity, has an aesthetic continuity that is undergirded by the experience of deep sorrow followed by great joy. That is, if you will, the *culture* of jazz music. The word culture itself is worthy of considerable elaboration. Human culture began with the Lord's command in Genesis 1:26 for humans to spread over the face of the earth and exercise gentle lordship over it.[2] One of the best succinct definitions of culture is by social historian Orlando Patterson: "By culture I mean a repertoire of socially transmitted and intra-generationally generated ideas about how to live and make judgments, both in general terms and in regard to specific domains of life."[3] Jazz is a culture that is both rich and varied, and yet somehow united. An important feature of that culture is not only the suffering and pain that is expressed in the music, but the intense joy—indescribable joy, a joy that is perhaps only capable of being articulated through music. In this concluding chapter, then, I would like to highlight seven joyful features of this music. We might call them the seven joys of jazz.

BLUESY

Jazz isn't jazz without a bluesy ambiance. This is its first joy. What do we mean by this trait? As previously noted, the blues expressed the tragedy,

---

[2]See William Edgar, *Created and Creating: A Biblical Theology of Culture* (Downers Grove, IL: IVP Academic, 2016).

[3]Orlando Patterson, "Taking Culture Seriously: A Framework and Afro-American Illustration," in *Culture Matters: How Values Shape Human Progress*, ed. Lawrence E. Harrison and Samuel P. Huntington (New York: Basic Books, 2000), 208.

pain, and loss of Black people, stolen from their homeland, suffering at the hands of those who inexcusably thought them less than human, yearning for freedom. Hundreds of years of oppression are expressed in the blues and the bluesy aspects of jazz. In his chapter on the origins of Delta blues in his book, *Looking Up at Down*, historian William Barlow describes the first blues: "The rural blues were a vocal music used to articulate the personal and social concerns that arose in the daily lives of African Americans."[4] The blues were varied, but the most standard arrangement involved a simple AAB form, with notes appropriately stretched and drawn-out, using what we call "blue notes," the flatted third, flatted fifth, and flatted seventh. Such abstract descriptions do not, of course, come near to conveying the passion and heartache of good blues.[5] Jazz at its best is never far from the blues. It may be pure blues or may involve the abstract sounds of a composition that is only distantly related to the blues.[6] But there must be a blues feeling in the mix.

STRENGTH TO CLIMB

The second joy is that of strength. As we have seen, jazz is the music of Black history, Black musicians—indeed, the whole Black experience and community. From the beginning, this has meant a struggle for recognition. There are many reasons this struggle was often rebuffed, but it was sometimes rewarded. The sad reality is that oppression often births opportunity. Sometimes, in the most difficult, demanding, and even dehumanizing of circumstances, humans can create truly amazing things. During and after slavery, that struggle against oppression somehow highlighted the unique contributions Black people were able to make, including jazz. W. E. B. Du Bois put it as well as anyone: the end of the

---

[4]William Barlow, *Looking Up at Down: The Emergence of Blues Culture* (Philadelphia: Temple University Press, 1989), 4.

[5]Listen, for example, to the plaintive urban sounds of Bobby Blue Bland: "This Time I'm Gone For Good," YouTube video, 3:33, posted by "Bobby 'Blue' Bland – Topic," July 31, 2018, www.youtube.com/watch?v=XXsz_coky5U. Heartbreaking!

[6]Take Duke Ellington's "Caravan" with its zany chords: "Duke Ellington – Caravan," YouTube video, 5:29, posted by "nina katsiashvili," January 24, 2010, www.youtube.com/watch?v=YkLBSLxo5LE.

African American's striving was "to be a co-worker in the kingdom of culture, to escape both death and isolation, to husband and use [the Negro's] best powers and his latent genius."[7] During Reconstruction and the migrations to the north, this husbanding translated into music styles. New ones were brought together: ragtime, blues, and eventually, jazz. One of the essential, nonnegotiables of jazz is its resilience. Sometimes it takes the form of protest. At other times, simply survival. But there is always an element of strength in the music that gives it its freshness.

INVENTION

Jazz is heavily based on improvisation. This is its third joy. The best jazz is simply inventive. A personal anecdote here might serve. When we lived in France, I was often called on to translate for various performing groups that came through. Naturally, this was a great delight since I was able to attend the numerous concerts. Once in Marseille the guest artists were the Stars of Faith of the Black Nativity, featuring Frances Steadman and Esther Ford. After a marvelous concert, we were in the backstage green room awaiting instruction for the late-night supper. It was a bit of a wait so the women started singing, spontaneously, something like "Lord, I'm hungry, when can we eat?" They kept adding verses and thickening the harmony. Of course, no such song was in the repertoire because it was entirely made up. I wish I had had a recording device. It was a one-off. But if the late-night request for food seems purely spontaneous, it wasn't. A number of unspoken and unscripted conventions went into the song. As discussed, various song lists and traditional pieces are known to every jazz musician, but each one brings his own or her own variations to them. Thus, when we hear Louis Armstrong or pianist Erroll Garner playing familiar tunes, they do it in their own distinctive styles. But they are drawing on established patterns.

Improvisation at its best is not simply theme and variation but telling a story. An anecdote relayed to me years ago told of two trumpeters, one older and one younger, who went to check out a phenomenal new talent,

---

[7]W. E. B. Du Bois, *The Souls of Black Folk* (Chicago: A. C. McLung, 1903), 13.

Roy Eldridge. After several numbers, the younger one said to his friend, "I think Roy has the best technique of any trumpet player alive." To which his companion said, "Yes, that's true, but he hasn't yet learned to tell a story." There are many talented musicians on the scene even today. Their technique can bowl you over. But not all of them tell a story in their sequencing of episodes within a tune. Apparently the two men went back several years later, and they agreed that Roy now could tell a story.

What does this mean? Among other things it means starting off with the "head," playing the piece simply, and then building and building until a climax is reached, and then coming back down. There are many other ways to tell a story. One involves conversations with the other musicians in the group. Another is to have a refrain (similar to a *ritornello* in classical music), which punctuates the story in key places. Another is the use of flashbacks. This is not unlike telling tales in literature. The marvelous American poet John Ciardi likens music to a poem, in contrast with an essay:

> The essay has satisfied its essential requirements when it has followed the facts—facts, opinions, argument, all in general that it "has to say." Music, on the other hand, follows itself, the first sound calling the second into being, and it the third, and so on until those inner calls become feelingly involved and feelingly solve themselves. Music has no fact. It is its own fact.[8]

The simplest kind of narrative is one that develops and progresses.

For but one example, the "Honky Tonk Train Blues" is constructed in this way.[9] A bit more complex is when themes are presented, turned around, and revisited. McCoy Tyner's version of the classic "Just in Time" demonstrates this.[10] After a brief introduction, there are three choruses for piano and rhythm, then a bass solo, then a section where the drums

---

[8]John Ciardi, *How Does a Poem Mean?* (Boston: Houghton Mifflin, 1959), 769.

[9]"Mead Lux Lewis plays 'Honky Tonk Train Blues'," YouTube video, 2:23, posted by "gullivior," August 13, 2022, www.youtube.com/watch?v=tDuLezFRMNU.

[10]"McCoy Tyner - JUST IN TIME," YouTube video, 6:05, posted by "Erlendur Svavarsson," February 14, 2014, www.youtube.com/watch?v=CTnNFlxe4kM. "Just in Time" is a popular tune written by Jule Styne and Betty Comden with Adolph Green. It was featured in the musical *Bells Are Ringing* in 1956. For those who are interested, this version has been

and piano "trade fours," and finally, back to the "head" and a coda.[11] Because Tyner's chords are thick, it is easy to miss the simplicity of the three choruses. In typical fashion, Tyner alternates these thick chords with simple, flowing lines. But the listener is never uninterested because, as Ciardi says, the first calls the second into being, and so forth. In the second chorus, the fluid melodic lines are intensified, and subtle syncopation is introduced. In the third, chords and lines become more complex, often using triplets. That intensifies and introduces the bass solo. Then, back to the top, followed by a special coda (a bit like the cadenza in a classical concerto). It ends with what we call a "tag," using a deceptive cadence several times then the end. In this way, it tells a story.

Improvisation also includes using traditional instruments in new ways. I am a pianist. I have often heard classical pianists (whom I envy) listening to me and saying they can't do that! There are method books and transcriptions but unless they are played with the right kind of earthiness, they aren't quite the real thing. Some instruments which had hitherto been just for cameos became the most prominent in jazz. This is the case of the saxophone, which was patented in 1846 by the Belgian Adolphe Sax and used sparsely in various orchestras. The clarinet was older still but became transmuted in the hands of New Orleans musicians. The double bass, though also ancient, became a necessary foundation for much of jazz, particularly played pizzicato.[12]

SWING

A fourth joy of jazz is the elusive concept of swing. Most fans know when it's there (or isn't), but it is quite difficult to define in words. When trumpeter Cootie Williams was asked to define swing, he apparently retorted, "Define

---

transcribed quite faithfully by Bob Leso, *McCoy Tyner: Jazz Giants* (Milwaukee: Hal Leonard, 1992), 56-70.

[11] A "chorus" is an iteration of the "head" which is the basic tune plus harmonies. In this case, each chorus is thirty-two measures long. A "trade" is when one instrument takes turns with another, often for four measures at a time, in this case being doubled to eight measures.

[12] For more on improvisation, see Bruce Ellis Benson, *Liturgy as a Way of Life: Embodying the Arts in Christian Worship* (Grand Rapids, MI: Baker Academic, 2013).

it, I'd rather tackle Einstein's theory."[13] Swing makes you want to move, either inwardly or explicitly. While inadequate, we can note that most swing is produced by emphasizing the second and the fourth beats in a four-beat measure. Generally, one can tell an inexperienced (often White) audience when asked to clap with a song. They will do it on the first and third beats.

One of the swingingest pianists is the great Erroll Garner. He characteristically sets up a rhythm in his left hand and then plays the tune with his right. He then ventures into the far reaches of melodic inventio, never far from the original tune, yet playing around its edges. His dexterity is astonishing. His swing is nearly inimitable. He can play as well as James P. Johnson and Willie "the Lion" Smith. Most often the swing rhythm is understated. The master of such understatement is no doubt Count Basie. His "C Jam Blues," played on piano over an orchestra and in dialogue with Ella Fitzgerald's scat singing, followed by successive solos over the steady beat of the drum, demonstrates this feature.[14] For an easier litmus test, listen to jazz. Ask yourself whether it moves you, outwardly or inwardly, to want to swing and dance. If not, then it may not be real jazz.

SOLIDARITY

The fifth joy of jazz is what you might call conversation. Jazz represents collective individualism. When jazz is played in groups there should always be a conversation between the musicians. Even a solo number converses with itself or with the tradition of jazz greats. In his thoughtful book, *The Contradictions of Jazz*, Paul Rinzler highlights four contradictions (I might have called them paradoxes) characteristic of jazz: (1) individualism and interconnectedness, (2) assertion and openness, (3) freedom and responsibility, and (4) creativity and tradition.[15] Upon reflection, these are but different ways of saying the same thing. One of the greatest joys in a good jazz performance is to watch the musicians

---

[13]"Swing (jazz performance style)," Wikiwand, www.wikiwand.com/en/Swing_(jazz_performance_style).

[14]"Ella Fitzgerald, Count Basie etc: C Jam Blues," YouTube video, 11:05, posted by "shanelee-brown," January 24, 2012, www.youtube.com/watch?v=J1_WJf6eDPE.

[15]Paul Rinzler, *The Contradictions of Jazz* (Lanham, MD: Scarecrow, 2008), 18.

commune with one another. This doesn't always happen in the same way, and it is certainly not scripted. But when the pianist looks up at his bass player and smiles, there is nothing quite like it.

FOLK TO GREAT ART

As we have noted, jazz began with rural folk roots, which gives jazz its sixth joy. Many jazz musicians began in the Mississippi Delta, and moved to New Orleans, before going north. But the music never lost its earthiness. Even in the polished compositions of Duke Ellington, there remain roots in the soil of the Black experience. Well before the advent of the marching bands and concert performances, there were family bands. Many families in places like Louisiana created bands with family members plus neighbors, and some became quite well-known. Perhaps the most famous musician who started out as a child in a family affair was trombonist Edward "Kid" Ory (1886–1973). He grew up on the Woodland Plantation in La Place, Louisiana. As a child (thus "Kid") in the 1890s he organized a "humming band" with his playmates. They would stand on a bridge and harmonize their four- or five-part singing. This little ceremony imitated the services of the Black churches. These children would create their own instruments, and they went around to baseball games and picnics and earned a few dollars as entertainers. In a word, they were innovators. Ory's trombone style came eventually to define the role of this instrument in the twentieth century.[16]

Eventually, jazz would expand into elaborate forms. A good deal happened between the rural blues and the concert stage. Miles Davis might sound far from the roots, but he never is. Consider his abstract work, "It's About That Time."[17] The musicians each appear to be on their own journey.

---

[16]Much of the information on Ory is documented in the Tulane Jazz Oral History Project, located at the William Ransom Hogan Jazz Archive at Tulane University. I have had the privilege of visiting that deposit and was much relieved to discover it was not affected by Hurricane Katrina, which devastated so much of the town. Also, there is a solid biography of Ory: John McCusker, *Creole Trombone: Kid Ory and the Early Years of Jazz* (Jackson: University Press of Mississippi, 2012).

[17]"Miles Davis - It's About That Time/The Theme (Live In Copenhagen, 1969)," YouTube video, 20:03, posted by "Miles Davis," March 27, 2020, www.youtube.com/watch?v=_CIZr5vH-m4.

But in fact, the music is an artful conversation. And it provides a setting for Miles's poem by the same title. There are allusions to rock, to jazz, and to space music here that invite the listener to reflect on the influence of the past on the present. This is jazz as art at the highest level.

THE GOSPEL

The seventh and final joy in jazz is the heart of the argument of the present volume: the influence of the Christian message. As I have argued, this inspiration was often indirect, more felt than articulated, but there were also explicit references to the Christian faith in the repertoire. More importantly, though, is the deep resonance between the good news of Jesus Christ, according to which the power, mercy, and grace of God is revealed in the life, death, and resurrection of Christ (Rom 1:16-17), and the movement from sorrow to joy found in jazz. The Christian message undeniably contains elements of both deep sorrow (Christ's prayer in the garden and of course his own suffering and crucifixion) as well as indescribable joy (his resurrection from the dead and his victory over sin and death). It is this narrative of God's love that pervades every musical aspect related to jazz. Lawrence Levine once stated, "The sacred world view so central in black slaves [involved] an intimate relationship between the world of sound and the world of sacred time and space."[18] He went on to argue that this connection would be severed in the twentieth century with the advent of secularization. This is no doubt true, and yet all kinds of vestiges are present in even the most abstract sorts of jazz.

To take but one example, the trumpeter Herman Autrey was raised in central Alabama and, as was typical, was integrated into the Christian faith, hard work, and a sense of community.[19] In his oral history, he explains that on the cotton fields, "someone would start the song, and they would all chime in, and you never heard such a thing in your life, such

---

[18]Lawrence Levine, *Black Culture and Black Consciousness* (New York: Oxford University Press, 2007), 158.

[19]Much of the information on Autrey and other local band leaders is found in the Smithsonian Jazz Oral History project, housed at the Institute of Jazz Studies at Rutgers University.

sounds, such harmonies." He added, "The music began after workers related stories to one another, like reading the paper . . . and then we'd go
into a religious theme," which led to more singing. From there, there was
a natural transition to performing music in the church, where all the
people were "together, singing, shaking hands, praying."[20]

My belief is that jazz cannot be understood apart from its relationship
to (and Black people's larger relationship with) the Christian faith. This is
the rhythm that plays in the music of jazz—sometimes quietly, sometimes
clearly, but always present. It is its greatest joy.

NO GREATER LOVE

In closing, we move from God's love to our own love for jazz.

We live for what we love. You may have heard the rhetorical question,
"Do we love to live or do we live to love?" In the best of cases, it should be
both. But surely living to love is better. James K. A. Smith tells us "You Are
What You Love."[21] I think the point is rather profound. He challenges us
to see whether our inmost desires are consistent with our confession, and
the measure of that is the set of daily habits we practice.[22]

Do we love jazz music? Here is the test to answer that question: Do I
listen to it, frequent it, make efforts to encounter it? Introduce friends to
it? This is not meant as a guilt trip for those whose commitment to jazz is
less than wholehearted or whole-souled. It is meant as a simple test. Have
I at least given it a chance? Growing to love jazz may take a lifetime. Yet it
moves—and moves us—from deep misery to inextinguishable joy. There
is no greater love. A supreme love!

---

[20]Harman Autrey Oral History Interview, Tape 3, https://ijsresearch.libraries.rutgers
  .edu/search-results?q1=%22Autrey%2C+Herman%22&q1field=facet:interviewee&key
  =7Mn2Sv5Dx.
[21]James K. A. Smith, *You Are What You Love* (Grand Rapids, MI: Brazos, 2016).
[22]Smith, *You Are What You Love*, 29.

APPENDIX

SELECTED JAZZ RECORDINGS

The following list of YouTube links is provided to help readers *hear* what they have been reading. It is necessarily selective. The first part draws from the examples cited in the text. A brief supplementary list is then proposed.

As I have noted above, jazz is a rather broad genre of music. As an inspiration to the reader, I must point out that there is a relative wealth of recordings along with some filmed testimony to which we may have access. There are hundreds of thousands of YouTube videos, as well as CDs, MP3s, and the like. A word of caution: while we should be deeply grateful for the abundance of such resources, much of it amounts to sampling and compressing audio, rather than providing the full context of a larger record. That represents an impoverishment, in the same way a glossy photo of a painting in a museum or a home is a poor representation of the real thing. Even better, of course, is attending a concert or a live show. There's nothing like it! The next best option is to view a documentary which shows a real set of performances. Though it suffers from various limitations, a good place to begin is Ken Burns's *Jazz* (DVD box set, 2005).

ORIGINS

(The New Orleans funeral) Dr. Michael White and Gregg Stafford. *Praying and Swaying*, vol. 1, "At the Cross." Recorded 2001. Audio recording of compact disc. www.jazzcrusade.com/JCCD/JC3062.html.

(Improvisation) "Oscar Peterson - C Jam Blues." YouTube video, 9:06, from a performance in Denmark in 1964 with Ray Brown (Bass) and Ed Thigpen (Drums). Posted by "dgbailey777," December 13, 2010, www.youtube.com /watch?v=NTJhHn-TuDY.

(Improvisation) "Joe Pass - 'Ain't Misbehavin'." YouTube video, 5:51, from a performance televised by BBC in 1993. Posted by "dave gould," July 23, 2014, www.youtube.com/watch?v=p_kUJa1PueM.

"Slave Ship Sound Effects/Images." YouTube video, 3:00, from the background of a performance excerpt from Amiri Baraka's "Slave Ship" at UCSB on May 1, 2013. Posted by "rectifiERIN," May 1, 2013, www.youtube.com/watch?v =fIg-e7jiug0.

"Bessie Griffin in concert 1972 (sometimes I feel like a motherless child)." YouTube video, 7:22, from a performance with the Johnny Thompson Singers in 1972. Posted by "Thejazzsingers channel," April 2, 2010, www.youtube.com/watch?v =8jaQjFs-gEY.

"Louis Armstrong 'Dinah' 1933." YouTube video, 2:52, from a performance with his band in Copenhagen in 1993. Posted by "harryoakley," March 3, 2009, www.youtube.com/watch?v=BhVdLd43bDI.

"Choir Boy Music Video: I Couldn't Hear Nobody Pray." YouTube video, 0:53, from a trailer for a Broadway play in 2018. Posted by "Manhattan Theatre Club," December 11, 2018, www.youtube.com/watch?v=3DPNJsvi8WQ.

"Roots of Blues - Lead Belly 'Rock Island Line'." YouTube video, 2:55, audio recording from 1944. Posted by "Literatisch," July 18, 2008, www.youtube.com /watch?v=lCiJ4QQG9WQ.

"Joe Savage's field holler: I woke up soon one morning (1978)." YouTube video, 1:03, audio recording from 1978. Posted by "Alan Lomax Archive," April 20, 2011, www.youtube.com/watch?v=1bRt-SI9bfw.

"Callie Day & Lan Wilson - I Know The Lord Will . . ." YouTube video, 4:40, from a performance of "I Know the Lord Will Make a Way," at First African Baptist Church, sung by Calesta Day with Landen Wilson (piano) in 2014. Posted by "Landen Wilson," August 16, 2014, www.youtube.com/watch?v=6RCQ TiCm2ac.

"Cab Calloway - Minnie the Moocher." YouTube video, 2:58, from a performance in 1958. Posted by "moontreal," March 18, 2008, www.youtube.com/watch?v =8mq4UT4VnbE.

SPIRITUALS

"Blind Willie Johnson - Dark Was the Night." YouTube video, 3:21, audio recording from 1927. Posted by "jovauri," August 7, 2007, www.youtube.com/watch?v=BNj2BXW852g.

"Big mama Thornton 'Go Down Moses.'" YouTube video, 4:35, audio recording with images from 1965. Posted by "anthony berrot," February 12, 2010, www.youtube.com/watch?v=CTZ4VyhLZOY.

"Swing Low Sweet Chariot - Fisk Jubilee Singers (1909)." YouTube video, 4:05, audio recording with images from 1909. Posted by "Nathaniel Jordon," December 23, 2012, www.youtube.com/watch?v=GUvBGZnL9rE.

"Three Mo' Tenors - Were You There - 7/17/2001 (Official)." YouTube video, 4:42, from a performance on July 17, 2001. Posted by "Jazz on MV," September 23, 2014, www.youtube.com/watch?v=uhGYD1svTM4.

"He Never Said a Mumblin' Word (Crucifixion)." YouTube video, 6:07, audio recording of Mose Hogan, Darryl Taylor, and Brent McMunn (piano), released on January 1, 2011. Posted by "Darryl Taylor - Topic," February 8, 2015, www.youtube.com/watch?v=_b-LxV4MuiI.

"Louis Armstrong - Nobody Knows (1962)." YouTube video, 2:32, from a performance in 1962. Posted by "wenturiano," August 24, 2007, www.youtube.com/watch?v=SVKKRzemX_w.

"Steal Away-Mahalia Jackson & Nat King Cole from Emeless." YouTube video, 4:47, from Nat King Cole's television show in 1957. Posted by "Emeless," November 29, 2006, www.youtube.com/watch?v=-O5hz5KnSdc.

GOSPEL

"'Oh Happy Day' Edwin Hawkins - Anthony Brown w/ FBCG Combined Choir." YouTube video, 6:35, from service at First Baptist Church of Glenarden. Posted by "Inside FBCG," February 14, 2018, www.youtube.com/watch?v=olQrCfkvbGw.

"MAHALIA JACKSON PRECIOUS LORD TAKE MY HAND." YouTube video, 5:03, from a performance in 1955. Posted by "Thejazzsingers channel," June 18, 2009, www.youtube.com/watch?v=as1rsZenwNc.

"Spirit of Memphis Quartet - Ease My Trouble In Mind." YouTube video, 2:32, audio recording with image) from 1951 recording. Posted by "Sliptrail," July 31, 2016, www.youtube.com/watch?v=Ex1WMFBLviY.

"HANDEL'S MESSIAH A SOULFUL CELEBRATION - And The Glory Of The Lord." YouTube video, 4:00, audio recording from 1992 of the song

"And the Glory of the Lord," from Handel's *Messiah*, on the album *A Soulful Celebration*. Posted by "kamedil," January 23, 2011, www.youtube.com/watch?v =6GTTdfgk570.

"Little Walter My Babe." YouTube video, 2:34, audio recording from album in 1955. Posted by "Angel Neira," April 11, 2009, www.youtube.com/watch?v=duRp _avXtMM.

"Bessie Smith - Saint Louis Blues, 1925." YouTube video, 3:15, audio recording with images of Bessie Smith with Louis Armstrong (cornet) and Fred Longshaw (harmonium) from 1925. Posted by "240252," March 24, 2012, www.youtube .com/watch?v=3rd9IaA_uJI.

"Joe Thomas - My Baby Done Left Me (1949)." YouTube video, 2:48, audio re-cording from 1949. Posted by "Overjazz," October 7, 2012, www.youtube.com /watch?v=x7BMImgCjNc.

"Cross Road Blues - Robert Johnson (1936)." YouTube video, 2:30, audio recording from 1936. Posted by "Nathaniel Jordan," February 3, 2013, www.youtube.com /watch?v=GtDlZdhHRCI.

"The Black Network~Nina Mae McKinney~Half of Me Wants to be Good~1936~pt 1/4." YouTube video, 4:05, from a performance on the Black Network in 1936. Posted by "preservationhall01," March 18, 2019, www.youtube .com/watch?v=K_3l5Q50d-s.

"Blind Gary Davis - Death Don't Have No Mercy." YouTube video, 4:15, from a performance in 1960. Posted by "duke ellington," September 12, 2018, www.youtube.com/watch?v=v1BvK_00loQ.

"Preachin' The Blues SON HOUSE (1930) Delta Blues Guitar Legend." YouTube video, 3:04, audio recording from 1930. Posted by "RagtimeDorainHenry," April 13, 2009, https://youtu.be/IpWh8vohjG4.

"Big Bill Broonzy - Key to the Highway." YouTube video, 3:02, audio recording from 1940 with Jazz Gillum (harmonica) and Washboard Sam (washboard). Posted by "KouKlouvahata Puppet Theatre," February 17, 2011, www.youtube .com/watch?v=KN_f0WVsHuw.

"Muddy Waters - Gypsy Woman (1948)." YouTube video, 2:35, audio recording from 1948 with Sunny Land Slim. Posted by "77GhettoD," March 31, 2011, www.youtube.com/watch?v=L8v3jtL1S6k.

"Mead Lux Lewis plays 'Honky Tonk Train Blues.'" YouTube video, 4:19, from a performance recorded in 1940, original song released in 1929. Posted by "gullivior," August 13, 2012, www.youtube.com/watch?v=tDuLezFRMNU&list =RDMM&index=5.

RAGTIME–STRIDE

"Maple Leaf Rag Played by Scott Joplin." YouTube video, 2:45, audio recording from 1899. Posted by "TJaep," October 19, 2006, www.youtube.com/watch?v =pMAtL7n_-rc.

"Fats Waller - Ain't Misbehavin' - Stormy Weather (1943)." YouTube video, 2:46, from a performance in 1943. Posted by "Bessjazz," November 6, 2009, www.youtube.com/watch?v=PSNPpssruFY.

"Carolina Shout - James P. Johnson (1921)." YouTube video, 2:43, audio recording from 1921. Posted by "Nathaniel Jordan," February 15, 2013, www.youtube.com /watch?v=wwhy5zxrAKI.

"Art Tatum - Yesterdays 1954." YouTube video, 2:17, from a performance in 1954. Posted by "masterofsynapsis," October 12, 2012, www.youtube.com/watch?v =q0QD558TWSQ.

EARLY JAZZ

"James Reese Europe 'Memphis Blues' Pathe recording 1919 W. C. Handy DEATH OF JIM EUROPE." YouTube video, 3:00, audio recording from 1919 with images. Posted by "Tim Gracyk," March 25, 2016, www.youtube.com/watch?v =2Eca4woBHzA.

"Original Dixieland Jass Band - Livery Stable Blues (1917)." YouTube video, 3:10, audio recording from 1917. Posted by "peppopb," November 2, 2007, www.youtube.com/watch?v=5WojNaU4-kI.

"Riverside Blues— King Oliver 1923." YouTube video, 2:51, audio recording from 1923 of Joe "King" Oliver's Creole Jazz Band. Posted by "erwigfilms," February 27, 2008, www.youtube.com/watch?v=j_WbQYdQty0.

"Louis Armstrong - West End Blues - Chicago, 28 June 1928." YouTube video, 3:15, audio recording from June 28, 1928. Posted by "Heinz Becker," June 16, 2011, www.youtube.com/watch?v=zPgh7nxTQT4.

"Georgia Swing - Jelly Roll Morton & His Red Hot Peppers (1928)." YouTube video, 2:27, audio recording from performance on June 11, 1928, in Liederkranz Hall in New York. Posted by "Atticus Jazz," September 23, 2020, www.youtube.com /watch?v=etiqFMKeK60.

"It Don't Mean a Thing (If It Ain't Got That Swing) - Duke Ellington & His Famous Orchestra (1932)." YouTube video, 3:08, audio recording from 1932 with images. Posted by "djbuddylovecooljazz," September 9, 2009, www.youtube.com /watch?v=-FvsgGp8rSE.

"Duke Ellington - Jungle Nights in Harlem." YouTube video, 3:04, audio recording from 1930. Posted by "OnlyJazzHQ," February 13, 2013, www.youtube.com /watch?v=PPVlxa2kgjg.

TOWARD THE MODERN

"Chick Webb & his Orchestra 5/18/1934 'Stompin' at the Savoy." YouTube video, 3:20, audio recording of a performance on May 18, 1934, with images. Posted by "thecrippledrummer," August 27, 2018, www.youtube.com/watch?v=Fuso2 MVwZlg.

"Caldonia / Louis Jordan." YouTube video, 2:53, from a performance in 1945. Posted by "Elwood Yodogawa," August 28, 2008, www.youtube.com/watch?v =PR6pHtiNT_k.

"A Night In Tunisia." YouTube video, 5:24, audio recording of Dizzy Gillespie performing "A Night in Tunisia." Posted by "Dizzy Gillespie - Topic," August 14, 2018, www.youtube.com/watch?v=eQHpwnXf0mI.

"Charlie Parker - The Bird." YouTube video, 4:46, audio recording with images from a recording session at Carnegie Hall in New York in December 1947 with Charlie "Bird" Parker Quartet. Posted by "charlieparkerjazzart," February 2012, www.youtube.com/watch?v=KYQCwoas3rk.

"Miles Davis - Blue In Green (Official Audio)." YouTube video, 5:38, audio recording from 1959. Posted by "Miles Davis," May 14, 2013, www.youtube.com /watch?v=TLDflhhdPCg.

THE GOSPEL IN JAZZ

"Sister Rosetta Tharpe- 'Didn't It Rain?' Live 1964 (Reelin' In The Years Archive)." YouTube video, 4:15, from a performance in 1964. Posted by "ReelinInTheYears66," December 27, 2017, www.youtube.com/watch?v=Y9a49oFalZE.

"Come Sunday (from Black, Brown, And Beige." YouTube video, 5:46, audio recording of Duke Ellington and his orchestra from 1958 (original recording in 1943). Posted by "Duke Ellington - Topic," February 20, 2017, www.youtube .com/watch?v=_FQv-BzZZbI.

"St. Martin de Porres." YouTube video, 6:36, audio recording of Mary Lou Williams from 1963. Posted by "Mary Lou Williams - Topic," May 21, 2015, www.youtube .com/watch?v=I_LcpXEA0W4.

"The Lord's Prayer (feat. Damien Sneed and Chorale Le Chateau." YouTube video, 4:12, audio recording of Jazz at Lincoln Center Orchestra with Wynton Marsalis, Damien Sneed, Chorale Le Chateau at the Lincoln Center in 2013. Posted

by "Jazz at Lincoln Center Orchestra - Topic," March 17, 2016, www.youtube
.com/watch?v=HmlI-Fceshc.

"Nina Simone - I Wish I Knew How It Would Feel to Be Free (Official Audio)."
YouTube video, 3:10, audio recording released in 1967 of Nina Simone singing
Billy Taylor's song. Posted by "Nina Simone," November 4, 2016, www.youtube
.com/watch?v=inNBpizpZkE.

"Oscar Peterson - Hymn to Freedom." YouTube video, 6:53, from a performance
in Denmark in 1964 with Ray Brown (bass) and Ed Thigpen (drums). Posted
by "dgbailey777," December 13, 2010, www.youtube.com/watch?v=tCrrZ1
NnCuM.

"To Hope! A Celebration." YouTube video, 37:46, from the Boulder Chorale's per-
formance of Dave Brubeck's "To Hope! A Celebration," on May 15, 2016.
Posted by "Boulder Chorale," July 21, 2016, www.youtube.com/watch?v
=ZtfjhRo03m4.

A TRIBUTE TO SPIRITUALS AND GOSPEL

"Wade in the water - Charlie Haden and Hank Jones-Steal Away." YouTube video,
4:10, audio recording from 1995. Posted by "Darren King," December 12,
2011, www.youtube.com/watch?v=SdylMDmDu4U.

"Cyrus Chestnut - There's a Sweet, Sweet Spirit." YouTube video, 5:37, audio recording from 2017. Posted by "Jazz Everyday!," May 22, 2019, www.youtube
.com/watch?v=HJk2xPfDaXo.

"Renewal." YouTube video, 6:44, audio recording of Monty Alexander from the
album *Uplift* from 2011. Posted by "Monty Alexander - Topic," October 7,
2015, www.youtube.com/watch?v=t4GYA9TAGwI.

"Ben Tankard - The Blessing." YouTube video, 3:42, audio recording from the 2012
album *Full Tank*. Posted by "Ram Kyo," December 3, 2016, www.youtube.com
/watch?v=b-eiBl2-eEI.

"Charles Mingus - Wednesday Night Prayer Meeting." YouTube video, 5:35, audio
recording from 1960. Posted by "Erlendur Svavarsson," July 11, 2013,
www.youtube.com/watch?v=x1WQR8Ti1vk.

"John Coltrane A Love Supreme." YouTube video, 7:48, audio recording from 1964
with images. Posted by "Yousaxyting," January 21, 2011, www.youtube.com
/watch?v=lHUapMTgWD0.

"Battle Hymn of the Republic (Closing Scene of Modern Warrior LIVE)." YouTube
video, 1:40, from a performance by Dominick Farinacci. Posted by "Dominick
Farinacci," November 11, 2019, www.youtube.com/watch?v=bly86afevU8.

THE JOYS OF JAZZ

Here are a few recordings not mentioned in the text of *A Supreme Love* that readers might enjoy.

"Jaki Byard - Parisian Solos [FULL ALBUM]." YouTube video, 1:01:24, audio recording of the full album recorded on July 29, 1971. Posted by "Futura Marge," December 22, 2019, www.youtube.com/watch?v=tZg5Ljjncrg.

"'Press On' from Frederick Douglass Jazz Works." YouTube video, 11:20, from a performance by Ruth Naomi Floyd at Calvary Chapel at Biola University, La Miranda, California, in February 2020. Posted by "ruthnaomifloyd," July 22, 2020, www.youtube.com/watch?v=rnu3X65zQCw.

"Jazz Piano - Bill Evans - The Solo Sessions, Vol 1 [Full Album]." YouTube video, 41:57, audio recording of full album from 1989. Posted by "Jazz & Japan," March 31, 2016, https://youtu.be/MXK-InD7GBU.

"Donald Lambert - Pilgrim's Chorus (1941) | Stride piano solo." YouTube video, 2:40, audio recording from 1941. Posted by "BlueBlackJazz," September 24, 2009, www.youtube.com/watch?v=eHLGVl9Ek8E.

"'Summertime' (1945) Artie Shaw." YouTube video, 5:01, audio recording from 1945 with images. Posted by "Mike Zirpolo," October 10, 2016, www.youtube.com /watch?v=FilTMFDREKY&list=RDGsiKy_H1KUM&index=6.

"Aaron Diehl Trio: 'Round Midnight by Thelonious Monk." YouTube video, 8:02, from a performance at the Players Club, New York City, on April 21, 2010. Posted by "Aaron Diehl," July 14, 2010, www.youtube.com/watch?v=13fCTDcszg4.

"Django Reinhardt - Minor Swing - HD *1080p." YouTube video, 3:16, audio recording from Le Quintette Hot Club de France in 1937. Posted by "bray hann," March 28, 2013, https://youtu.be/gcE1avXFJb4.

"Ahmad Jamal - Autumn Leaves - Palais des Congrès Paris 2017 - LIVE HD." YouTube video, 11:50, from a performance at Palais des Congrès Paris in 2017. Posted by "Zycopolis TV," February 21, 2018, www.youtube.com/watch?v=xnW9wNN_IVg.

"Herb Ellis & Remo Palmer - Windflower (1978)." YouTube video, 40:08, audio recording of the album from 1978. Posted by "Pedro Nóbrega," November 11, 2018, www.youtube.com/watch?v=fAi7IeJG-6Y.

"Benny Goodman Orchestra - Sing, Sing, Sing." YouTube video, 3:10, from a performance. Posted by "Ifasul," September 13, 2014, www.youtube.com/watch?v =GwPvLMlGWPI.

"Thelonious Monk Quartet Live In 66 Norway & Denmark concerts." YouTube video, 1:01:36, from performances in Norway and Denmark. Posted by "colibri crazy," June 20, 2017, www.youtube.com/watch?v=5o59Nsw7wxU.

"Bud Powell - I Want To Be Happy (1961) Paris." YouTube video, 3:36, from a per-
    formance in Paris on July 1, 1961. Posted by "kadarkar b," March 12, 2017,
    www.youtube.com/watch?v=72vmRqayW0E.
"Ray Bryant 1977 - Django." YouTube video, 4:18, from a performance in Montreux,
    Switzerland, on July 13, 1977. Posted by "rujazz," July 25, 2014, www.youtube
    .com/watch?v=olUknJkFK-k.
"jazzahead! 2019 - Matthew Whitaker." YouTube video, 45:43, from a performance
    at the Jazz Ahead! Festival in Bremen, Germany, in 2019. Posted by "jazzahead-
    tradefair," April 27, 2019, www.youtube.com/watch?v=oKEZ3CgygF8.

IMAGE CREDITS

GENERAL INDEX

SCRIPTURE INDEX